D1382859

SUPREME NEGLECT

I N A L I E N A B L E  R I G H T S S E R I E S

. . .

Supreme Neglect

. . .

HOW TO REVIVE CONSTITUTIONAL

PROTECTION FOR PRIVATE PROPERTY

Richard A. Epstein

OXFORD
UNIVERSITY PRESS

2008

OXFORD

UNIVERSITY PRESS

Oxford University Press, Inc., publishes works that further
Oxford University's objective of excellence
in research, scholarship, and education.

Oxford   New York
Auckland   Cape Town   Dar es Salaam   Hong Kong   Karachi
Kuala Lumpur   Madrid   Melbourne   Mexico City   Nairobi
New Delhi   Shanghai   Taipei   Toronto

With offices in
Argentina   Austria   Brazil   Chile   Czech Republic   France   Greece
Guatemala   Hungary   Italy   Japan   Poland   Portugal   Singapore
South Korea   Switzerland   Thailand   Turkey   Ukraine   Vietnam

Copyright © 2008 by Oxford University Press, Inc.

Published by Oxford University Press, Inc.
198 Madison Avenue, New York, NY 10016

www.oup.com

Library of Congress Cataloging-in-Publication Data
Epstein, Richard Allen, 1943–
Supreme neglect : how to revive constitutional protection
for private property / Richard A. Epstein.
p. cm. — (Inalienable rights series ; v. 4)
Includes index.
ISBN 978-0-19-530460-2
1. Right of property—United States.
2. Constitutional law—United States.
3. Eminent domain—United States.
4. Land use—Law and legislation—United States. I. Title.
KF562.E67 2008   346.7304—dc22   2007032479

19.95

1 3 5 7 9 8 6 4 2

Printed in the United States of America
on acid-free paper

To
Bella Catherine Pianko
Our First Grandchild

Contents

. . .

CONTENTS

CONTENTS

[ix]

Editor's Note

. . .

> We hold these truths to be self-evident, that all men are created
> equal, that they are endowed by their Creator with certain
> unalienable Rights....
>
> —THE DECLARATION OF INDEPENDENCE

. . .

The Fifth Amendment to the United States Constitution provides, in part: "Nor shall private property be taken for public use
without just compensation." What does this mean? In this book,
Richard Epstein explores the meaning, constitutional import, and
institutional implications of the Takings Clause.

Like other provisions of the Bill of Rights, the takings clause is
not self-defining. What is "private property"? Does it include your
home, your land, the oil below your land, the air above it, your
ideas, a song you compose? What is a "taking"? Is a zoning restriction a "taking"? Suppose the city council passes a law prohi-
biting homeowners from using their property for commercial
purposes. Is that a "taking"? Is the income tax a "taking"? What is

"public use"? If the government may take your home in order to build a public highway or housing project (as long as it offers "just compensation"), may it also take your home in order to enable a private developer to build a shopping center?

What is "just compensation"? Does it include only the "fair market value" of your home, or your distinctive attachment to it? After all, you might not be willing voluntarily to sell your home for the "fair market value." Finally, are there circumstances in which the government may constitutionally take private property *without* paying just compensation? May the government order me to cut off branches of my tree that overhang my neighbor's property, without compensating me for the loss? What if cutting off the branches will kill my tree?

As Richard Epstein demonstrates, these questions are not only intellectually interesting, but profoundly important to our society. They have implications for the constitutionality of such legislative policies as progressive income taxation, estate and gift taxes, unemployment benefits, welfare, social security, labor law, price and rent controls, zoning ordinances, endangered species laws, land preservation statutes, oil and gas regulation, and so on. They affect almost every corner of American society.

Over the past seventy years, the Supreme Court has abandoned the strong version of the takings clause championed by the framers of the Fifth Amendment in favor of the much weaker version of the clause advocated by early twentieth-century Progressives and supporters of the New Deal. Epstein argues that "by yielding too much power to state regulation," the modern understanding of the takings clause decreases "social wealth and social welfare" and increases "the scope for factional politics that produce short-term advantages for some at the cost of long-term dislocations for society as a whole." These, he argues, are serious losses to the overall well-being of society.

Those who challenge Epstein's account, which he concedes is "out of the proverbial intellectual mainstream," will attack it as "an excuse for private selfishness and greed." But Epstein boldly and unapologetically responds that this criticism is profoundly off the mark. In fact, he maintains, the strong constitutional protection of private property is "a sound social institution." Legislation should not pass constitutional muster "if it works just for the rich and privileged, or indeed for any other discrete social group." Rather, he contends, "good legislation must create gains that are shared among all persons within the society." A central goal of his strong account of the takings clause is to limit the factional abuses that can distort any system of democratic politics and ensure that social innovations are, as he says, "win-win instead of win-lose propositions."

In *Supreme Neglect*, Epstein questions some of the most fundamental precepts of modern constitutional law and argues that "the faithful constitutional protection of private property is not some parochial exercise," but "an indispensable part of any comprehensive constitutional order that advances long-term social welfare." He maintains that just as a strong view of the freedom of speech and the freedom of religion is necessary to serve fundamental constitutional values, so, too, is a strong view of the takings clause. He offers here a powerful, provocative, and important challenge to the prevailing conception of private property in a free and democratic society.

February 2008   Geoffrey R. Stone

Preface

· · ·

Two Sets of Books

I THINK IT IS APPROPRIATE to offer a short autobiographical account of why and how I became interested in the constitutional protection of private property under the takings clause. The explanation lies, in an odd sense, in the peculiar path of my own education, which began with my exposure to Roman law and the common law while I was a student at Oxford University in the mid-1960s. The emphasis in an English education was on private law subjects. Private law covers only disputes between ordinary individuals, where the role of the government is to adjudicate and enforce the rights of the litigants and to lay down rules of more general application for future disputes.

Private law dominated those studies because the English have no written constitution, and thus offer no explicit, but some customary, protection against government deprivation of property. But the early study of the common-law rules convinced me that these rights had a utility, reach, and inner coherence that explained their wide acceptance not only in England but everywhere throughout the world, including the United States. The basic principles can be articulated in ways that remain functional across cultures and over time. When I completed my legal studies in the United States, the study of American constitutional law loomed large. Immediately, I was struck with the major transformation from the property-protective regime that had been championed by the framers of our Constitution to the weak property regimes championed by the Progressive politics of the early twentieth century, which were turned into constitutional law during the New Deal.

The most evident feature of the modern period is the sharp divergence between the private law of private property, which has developed with marvelous sophistication, and the crude and dismissive treatment private property receives in modern American constitutional law. It is as though there were two sets of books, with little in common between them. The private law of private property seeks to wring as much benefit out of all resources as is humanly possible. It leaves nothing to waste when it protects all sticks in the common-law bundle of rights, which include exclusive rights of possession, use, and disposition. The private law is sensitive to the exploitation of property by furnishing its owners with effective systems of recordation and transfer. And it builds in key limitations on the rights of one property owner to protect the like interests of his neighbor. The modern constitutional law does not seek to protect the full panoply of private rights, but tends, mistakenly, to extend a high level of protection solely to the right to exclude. It is as though the holder of an orange is entitled to exclusive possession of the rind, but needs government permission to use or dispose of the fruit that lies within.

This truncation of property rights is of no little consequence. If the private law governing private property is correct, then the public law, as developed in the Supreme Court's jurisprudence on the subject, is not. If, moreover, the private law works to maximize overall social welfare, then the current constitutional doctrines, by yielding too much power to state regulation, will decrease social wealth and social welfare by increasing the scope for factional politics that produce short-term advantages for some at the cost of long-term dislocations for society as a whole.

My purpose in writing this book is to show why, above all, private property is a sound social institution, and not just an excuse for private selfishness and greed. In doing so, I have incurred many obligations. The initial idea of writing this book was proposed to me by Dedi Felman, who was then an energetic and able acquisitions editor at the Oxford University Press; she was unsparing in her comments on an earlier draft. I also thank her successor in office, David McBride, who oversaw the final stages of production. The operative cause in this venture was my longtime University of Chicago colleague and friend Geoffrey Stone, who as series editor first asked me to write this book, and then proceeded to edit it sentence by sentence with his relentless black pen. As always, my redoubtable literary agent, and former student, Lynn Chu, has urged me to write more simply than I think myself able to do. Finally, I owe a true debt to my four research assistants, who plowed through the multiple versions of the text with an eye to making it as accessible as possible: Corina Wilder Davis, class of 2008, and Kayvan Noroozi, class of 2009, University of Chicago Law School; David Strandness, class of 2007, Stanford Law School; and Paul Laskow, class of 2009, New York University Law School.

The nature of this short book is shaped by the overall project. The effort to reach a popular audience meant that this book could not contain many of the familiar elements of the standard legal text. So it is useful to list all the things this book does *not* offer: a comprehensive overview of the entire area; a detailed analysis of the procedural issues in takings cases; a close reading of Supreme Court opinions; a discussion of the contrary views of the many able scholars who have worked in this area; an exploration of tangents into related areas; and, last but not least, any footnotes. The aim is for a short, crisp, and accessible exposition of the basic themes in this area, with a constant comparison of the differences between the approaches taken by the champions of small and large elements. Let it be no secret that I count myself firmly in the former camp. If readers are interested in how an analysis of private property and the Constitution can expand when all these elements are bought back in, I hope they will turn to two more academic books I have written on this subject: *Takings: Private Property and the Power of Eminent Domain* (1985) and *Bargaining with the State* (1993).

I am, of course, well aware that the views expressed in this book are out of the proverbial intellectual mainstream, for which I offer no apologies. Any errors in conception or execution are of course mine alone.

Hoover Institution   Richard A. Epstein
Stanford University, California   February 27, 2007

SUPREME NEGLECT

Introduction
. . .

Private Property, Then and Now

A RUDE PUBLIC AWAKENING

The institution of private property is as old as civilization itself. It's biologically ordained that we are all separate people who need both protection from the attacks of our enemies and the ability to cooperate with our families and friends. The system of private property allows us to achieve both of these goals simultaneously. The right to exclude protects against both conscious aggression and accidental entry. The rights to use and dispose of property facilitate coordination with other people. This trinity of exclusive possession, use, and disposition has long been recognized as forming the core of private property that lies at the center of organized social life. Its social importance helps explain why private property has been so vital to the organization of every legal system. Traditional legal thinkers in both the Roman law and common-law tradition constantly insisted on this key proposition: "property is the guardian of every other right." The logic that drives this expression is that only a system of private property lets people form and raise families, organize religious and other charitable organizations, and earn a living through honest labor.

Our founding fathers had a keen appreciation of the central role of private property in social life, which is why they included the "takings clause" in the Fifth Amendment to the United States Constitution: "Nor shall private property be taken for public use without just compensation." The evident partiality for limited government that animates that provision has not held firm throughout our nation's history. Indeed the revolution of Franklin D. Roosevelt's New Deal was made possible by the conscious choice of the United States Supreme Court to make sure the takings clause did not hamper or overturn any of Roosevelt's comprehensive legislative reforms, which imposed greater government control over the nation's economic activity. The Supreme Court's neglect of the takings clause has proved to be more important than its vigorous enforcement. The purpose of the book is to offer a roadmap for the revival of property rights in the United States and for the social improvement that this constitutional change should usher in.

The task, however urgent, does not enjoy widespread social support today. Generally speaking, but subject to notable exceptions, the New Deal reforms have received widespread approbation in both legal and popular circles. Over the past seventy years, most ordinary Americans, both liberal and conservative, have not considered private property as playing a key role in our constitutional order. To mention just one straw in the wind, even Republican administrations have not strongly supported the protection of property rights in the courts. Government policymakers on both sides of the aisle have been more concerned with the short-term impact of adverse decisions on the federal treasury than with any systematic analysis of the long-term social implications of legal regimes with weak property rights protection. Of course, people are proud to own their own homes and businesses, and they surely have an inchoate belief that the government may not ransack their premises or drive them out of their homes without cause. But, with the exception of a few stalwarts in a property rights movement that began to pick up steam in the Reagan years, the popular concerns with property have been personal—can I make my mortgage payments?—not theoretical or constitutional. For the past seventy years, the Progressive agenda of the New Deal has dominated social life: private property has not been part of the mainstream political agenda.

That popular complacency vanished in June 2005, when the U.S. Supreme Court handed down *Kelo v. City of New London*. Suddenly people could relate to homeowners who were cast out of their homes to facilitate "economic development." They could relate to Susette Kelo, the registered nurse who had purchased her Victorian house in 1997, or to Wilhelmina Dery, who shared the house in which she was born with her husband of fifty-nine years. They and perhaps a dozen others had their lives uprooted when the liberal wing of the Supreme Court, by a five-to-four margin, held that the city of New London could condemn their homes as part of a redevelopment plan for its faltering downtown. To be sure, the Court held that Kelo and her fellow homeowners held a constitutional right to "just compensation." But many people wondered whether our constitutional formula, or indeed any other formula, could fully compensate these property owners for the massive dislocations that government brought into their lives.

With *Kelo*, private property made a comeback on both sides of the political spectrum. Nationwide outrage on the political left and right followed in its wake. As of early 2007, thirty-four states had adopted constitutional or statutory reforms that sought to prohibit or limit state condemnations done to advance economic development. The issues quickly spilled over beyond the particulars of *Kelo* to spark a nationwide debate on property rights generally. A new generation of cynics wondered why we should trust Supreme Court justices on any issue if they are too obtuse to distinguish between public and private use, or even try. Conservatives saw *Kelo* as a creeping form of state socialism. Populists and communitarians saw the insidious hand of well-heeled private developers lurking in the background.

In this instance, the doomsayers have proved correct. As this is written, more than two years have passed since the Court handed down its decision in *Kelo*, and this is the situation on the ground. The entire 93-acre site remains vacant of any structures; Susette Kelo's house, the last structure standing, has been carted away as part of a compromise. Nonetheless, the city has built on schedule its ghostly infrastructure, complete with paved streets, new walkways, and historic-style lamps. The entire area is surrounded by an esplanade that leads to nowhere. No new construction is in sight. The project developers, Corcoran Jennison and the Coast Guard Museum (in honor of New London's maritime heritage), would each like the other to build first. It took more than six years to boot Kelo and her neighbors from their homes. It will likely take ten or fifteen years for construction to be completed.

Taken in isolation, *Kelo* looks like the train wreck many feared would happen. But let's slow down to look at the other side of the case. The larger issues do not turn solely on the plight of individual landowners; they have for centuries been forced to vacate their properties to allow the building of roads and courthouses. And it's worth recalling that both federal and state courts have permitted takings for some kinds of economic development for at least 150 years. Many critics excoriated the *Kelo* Court for the sin of judicial activism. But so long as that epithet signals the unwarranted intrusion of courts into matters best left to legislatures and local governments, this criticism gets the issue exactly backward. *Kelo*'s critics weren't trying to rein in a swashbuckling Supreme Court. To the contrary, they wanted the Court to take an activist stance by striking down a comprehensive plan that had survived endless rounds of public hearings. Yet just how far would they go? Would *Kelo*'s critics stick to their guns if New London condemned not private homes but a useless brownfield—land that can be developed only after soil pollutants have been removed—owned by multiple owners in order to sell it to a private developer for economic development?

TAKING THE LONGER VIEW

The purpose of these pointed questions is not to show that the critics of *Kelo* are wrong. They aren't. Rather, the point is to back off the dramatic particulars of individual cases in order to take a more patient, detached, and, above all, systematic view of a difficult subject, which has long suffered from the lack of any serious guidance from the Supreme Court. Takings law is complicated and it is technical. It is easy to go wrong in several directions at once. Why? Because—as with the other great constitutional guarantees of religion, free speech, due process, and equal protection—the shorter the text, the greater its hidden complexities. Necessarily, the written text of any open-ended constitutional provision raises more questions than it answers. Most modern statutes define their key operative terms. But our Constitution does not define "the freedom of speech," "due process of law," or "equal protection of the laws." And it certainly contains no definition of "private property," "take," "public use," or "just compensation." Like it or not, to figure out what these words mean we must turn to extrinsic material that runs the gamut from popular usage to historical practice and learned commentary.

We have lots of sources on these issues. We know that private property was a central institution of the European civil law tradition that started with the Roman law of Justinian, and of the English common-law tradition that started with the Norman Conquest. We know that the protection of private property from the Crown was a major purpose of the Magna Carta as early as 1215. Centuries later, the key writers who set the intellectual framework for our Constitution—John Locke, David Hume, William Blackstone, Adam Smith, and James Madison—all treated private property as a bulwark of the individual against the arbitrary power of the state.

There is, however, a vast difference between a keen appreciation of the need for private property and a systematic account of how to structure its protection. Lawyers and judges have to apply broad principles to a myriad of discrete situations that were nowhere in evidence when the Constitution was drafted. They have to learn to be faithful to the original constitutional design, while updating it to address new social realities. But even with all these social changes, we start with the constitutional text itself. In dealing with the takings clause, we have to track the text. First, we must give some account of "private property," which is one of the most complex social institutions in all cultures. Does it cover interests in land? Improvements? Water? Air? Patents? We must also decide what actions of government "take" private property. Must the government occupy the land? Are taxes takings? Third, we must ask when a taking is for a public use. Roads and forts are covered, but what about private railroads and hospitals? Finally, we must determine the level of just compensation. Is it only the fair market value of property? Does it cover Susette Kelo's distinctive psychological attachment to her own house?

Nor does the difficulty stop here, for key *non*textual elements, most notably the justifications for government action that go under the name of "the police power," have factored into the analysis to lend it some measure of intellectual coherence.

A longer explanation of the police power will have to wait, but this simple example introduces the problem: can the state take an axe from its owner if he is about to cut down someone else's tree? If so, must it pay compensation? If the answer to the first question is yes, and the second is no, then we open up a wide vista of interpretive issues that cannot be avoided by pretending, as the Supreme Court does, that the taking has not occurred. Fueled by countless examples, focused questions about the takings clause may be unanswerable without a solid grasp of the entire system of the property relationships governing ordinary private individuals. The constitutional inquiry grows inexorably and exponentially, even for theorists who think the key to constitutional interpretation lies in isolating the plain meaning of terms found in the text.

One can get some measure of the problem by noting the full range of legislative initiatives that have been challenged with only mixed success under the takings clause: progressive income taxation, estate and gift taxes, unemployment benefits, welfare, social security, workers' compensation statutes, collective bargaining laws, price and rent controls, zoning ordinances, endangered species laws, wetland statutes, landmark preservation statutes, mortgage moratoria, mining, oil and gas regulation, and on and on. Figuring out which of these laws should make sense and which do not is a genuine challenge. Some of these laws rest, sensibly enough, on the assumption that *monolithic* property rights lead to excessive prices and insufficient access. Other laws, sensibly enough, rest on the claim that *fragmented* property rights, such as oil and gas, or copyrights and patents, preclude the effective management of a single owner. There are, in fact, some sensible limitations that should be imposed on the rights to exclude, to use, and to dispose. Yet it hardly follows that either of these justifications works across the board for all kinds of resources where neither concentration nor fragmentation of resources is at issue.

The stakes are enormous. Follow the view of limited government in vogue in the founding period, and most (but not all) of the distinctive New Deal and Great Society reforms fall under a constitutional guillotine, a result that astounds—and dismays— most political thinkers and constitutional scholars, including all members of the current Supreme Court, both liberal and conservative. Take a more sympathetic view that sees government as a positive agent of public good, and the core protections of private property do not, and should not, block any major piece of social legislation that Congress, or the states, think are consistent with the advancement of the public good, as they see it. With only small differences, both liberal and conservative members of the Supreme Court embrace this positive vision of the regulatory state. The gap between the minimal state of the strong takings clause and the welfare state of the weak takings clause represents to this day our central constitutional chasm. Have we betrayed our constitutional heritage, or have we prudently adapted the Constitution to the changing realities of modern society?

Let me lay my cards on the table at the outset. The Supreme Court is guilty of massive neglect in its interpretation of the takings clause. As a matter of first principle, I take the decidedly unpopular view that the takings clause (and other constitutional provisions) commits this nation to a system of strong property rights and limited government. This view is at war with the major economic and social reforms of the New Deal and beyond. But do not overreact just yet: nothing in this view interferes with any efforts of the federal or state governments to provide those collective services. The state may raise taxes and impose regulations that stand a decent chance of advancing the overall social welfare, including establishing regulations that are needed to maintain social order, to build and maintain social infrastructure, and to constrain monopoly.

This strong reading of the takings clause, moreover, does not exalt the individual over the community. Rather, it insists that propositions about "the public," "society," or "the community" are not statements about organic groups that have value independent of the individuals who compose them. To the contrary, claims about the benefits and harms to society have to be broken down into statements about the benefits and harms to real people. Any judgment about how the community fares has to be decomposed into judgments about how any particular government initiative alters, up or down, the situations of all individuals, taken one at a time, within the group. Sometimes the outcome is easy to evaluate. If everyone benefits, then it is hard to deny that the community benefits as well. But sometimes some individuals gain while others lose: zoning and rent control are conspicuous examples. Bland statements that such legislation is good for the community suppress these inherent conflicts, and give no clue to their proper resolution.

One of my purposes in writing this book is to make good on the claim that a strong defense of private property and limited government does *not* rest on the parochial ambition to help the privileged few at the expense of society's most vulnerable members. Rather, a rigorous social perspective asks how legislation affects all individuals. Legislation should not pass muster if it works just for the rich and privileged, or indeed for any other discrete social group. Rather, good legislation must create gains that are shared among all persons within the society, ideally in proportion to their individual stakes. John F. Kennedy sounded the right note when he said that a rising tide raises all ships. Our constitutional structure should improve the odds of making social innovations win-win instead of win-lose propositions.

Viewed in this light, the takings clause is a key tool for reconciling two tasks. The first task is to provide collective goods—internal order, national defense, and social infrastructure—that are needed for social life. The second task is to control the endless interest-group struggles in which each faction champions those taxes and regulations that let it capture the lion's share of the social benefits from government action, while forcing its opponents to bear most, if not all, of its costs. The constitutional challenge is to create a government that is large enough to discharge its essential functions, without becoming so large as to destroy the property of those it must protect.

Before taking up the elaboration of the takings clause, I must address two central topics. First, we need to understand the history and role a system of private property plays in any legal system, including our own. So I shall track in broad outline the key stages in the development of private property from ancient times to today. This material about acquisition, protection, and disposition of property rights may seem far afield from contemporary constitutional law, but it is not. Each and every concept raised in this analysis plays a crucial role in any modern descriptive and normative constitutional analysis. The intellectual coherence of these concepts should not be undermined by putting them in quotation marks, or by giving them new meanings unrelated to their traditional usage. The building blocks of a thousand years have endured because they work.

The constitutional text offers a second signpost. Every word in the Constitution has to bear some appropriate meaning. Ignoring any of its terms means something is amiss. To be sure, it would be foolish to insist that all constitutional disputes have single correct answers. Any sound system of interpretation will have to grapple with hard cases. But the penumbra around twilight does not mean that night and day are artificial human constructions with no descriptive import. Our interpretive tools have to set the constitutional text within its larger legal and social context. There is no way to see how the Constitution regulates or protects private property without a clear grasp of how that system is put together and why it makes sense—issues to which I now turn.

Part I   Background Principles

CHAPTER ONE

Private Property

Its Origins, Structure, and Utility

PROPERTY: COMMON AND PRIVATE

Private property has been part of all human societies since primitive times. Long before the rise of the modern state, individuals had to distinguish between mine and thine, if only to decide who could eat what food, wear what clothes, carry what tools, and sleep in what place. To be sure, many primitive societies made their informal property allocations within clans or extended families and not by arm's-length exchanges between strangers. It is therefore difficult to extract much information about private property from these early practices. Instead we must content ourselves with a few imperfect generalizations. In hunter-gatherer societies, any territorial boundaries were probably stronger between tribes than between tribal members. Within extended clans, individual property rights probably attached more to the movables than to the land, which groups moved through but never occupied. Only when agriculture made it both necessary and profitable to clear the land for cultivation did strong property rights in land develop. Over time, these rights generated the modern state, which enjoys the monopoly of force within a given territory.

The first systematic accounts of private property are found in Roman law. Those rules, while largely limited to land and movables, show an immense sophistication, which has allowed them to survive in large measure to the present day. The key text is the *Institutes of Justinian*, whose opening salvo divided property into two types, common and private. The first included the air and water (and by extension, the beach), which are open with equal access to all comers. No private individual could remove these resources from the common for private use. More concretely, no individual could block, drain, divert, or pollute any body of water for private gain. In addition, common property included public buildings and arenas, as well as sensitive structures such as the walls of a city, which could not be divided without exposing the inhabitants to great risk from foreign enemies. Justinian doesn't talk about how to enforce these public rights. Instead he is content to justify their creation solely by reference to the laws of nature, which natural reason commends, he says, to civilized communities everywhere. Modern writers take a more functional approach. The effective use of water requires that many people share it at one time. How the sharing best takes place is hard to say abstractly, because much depends on the configuration of the waterway (a small river and a raging rapid have different uses) and the technological means available for its exploitation. But in general, the basic systems of water rights all seek some balance among consumption, navigation, recreation, and fishing. The law constantly speaks of correlative and reasonable uses, never absolute and exclusive dominion.

The Romans devoted far more effort to articulating the law of private property. Many of their views carried over first to

England, and from there to the United States. The first question related to property law lays the foundation for all that follows. How do any individuals have or gain rights in their own persons? Clearly the issue matters, because if persons are not free and equal in the state of nature, then slavery becomes a viable social option, as a lesser evil than death after conquest. With rare exceptions, people who are asked to choose which of two societies they would prefer to live in—without knowing their future social role—reject one in which they stand equal chance of being master and slave and prefer one that requires each person to respect the like liberty of others. That requirement carries with it the right to marry and perform productive labor, which become indisputable elements of personal liberty.

The takings clause does not protect personal liberty directly, for the private property in the Constitution refers chiefly to external objects: land, wildlife, or ordinary household possessions. Who owns them anyhow? Our legal system had this take on the question: in the state of nature, the earth and things on it were not owned by any human being. The first person to occupy land acquired ownership of it, at least if he marked off its boundaries to put the world on notice that he had taken it into possession. Wildlife and fish were acquired by capture, and other items like fruits were similarly acquired. The *unilateral* act of a single individual was universally judged sufficient to create ownership rights against the entire world, none of whom had consented to the acquisition.

From the outset, property theorists were vexed by this foundational feature. Locke rejected the easy solution of treating all property rights as a grant of God or the sovereign. Divine rights don't resonate in a world of religious differences, and who gave the sovereign its rights in the first place? Instead, Locke insisted that the labor of each individual, when added to an object found in nature, was sufficient to mark it off as his own. But his theory suffers from at least three serious defects. First, where does any person get the initial right to "mix" his labor with natural resources? Why can't others prevent his taking sole control of land, as they can for water? Second, even if the first possessor gets some rights, why should he get *every* right, as opposed to a limited interest equal to the added value of his labor? Third, Locke's view is in tension with the uniform historical practice, which simply assigned complete ownership to the first taker, without asking whether his labors were few or many, so long as he gave notice of his claim to the rest of the world, usually by fencing or recording. The ratio of labor to value is irrelevant.

Other writers sought to avoid Locke's quandary by invoking a theory of tacit consent. Hugo Grotius, a great Dutch theorist of the seventeenth century, thought that all persons impliedly consented to a rule that was self-evidently correct. Adam Smith thought that an "impartial observer" would recognize the special position of the first taker, so that the uniform consent of mankind could be inferred from the rationality of the rule. Blackstone invited his readers to choose between these two views, without taking sides.

The clue to resolving this dispute lies in Blackstone's terse remark "Necessity begat property." Historically, private property arose from a state of nature because no other system was workable. If the future owner needed consent (express or implied) from one stranger, then he needed it from all. Yet, as John Locke noted, everyone would starve if universal consent were needed before anyone could settle on a small plot of land or pick an acorn from a tree. Some individuals could not be found; some were unborn; and others would surely hold out for a huge payment. Express consent was out of the question. Implied consent was at best a helpful fiction. But necessity gives us the right focus. The dangers of unilateral acquisition—early and excessive consumption—were trivial compared to the massive paralysis that would ensue if no one could build, farm, or eat without the unanimous consent of everyone else. From the beginning, private property always rested on its productive advantage, and not merely on an obscure natural law claim that property rights are necessarily "immutable" across all times and places.

PRIVATE PROPERTY: THE UPSIDE

Yet if the intellectual foundations of the entire system were rickety, its consequences were both elegant and clear. All legal systems confer a handsome payoff on the original possessor of any natural resource: complete and indefinite ownership. The owner of land, for example, had what Blackstone called "sole and despotic dominion"—at the very least the right to exclude everyone in the world, not only from the surface of the land, but from the earth below (including minerals) to the heavens above (including building rights). An owner had the right to exclude others for an indefinite length of time, which ended only when the object owned was consumed or destroyed.

This right to exclude is no trivial matter, for it requires everyone else to forbear from entering, using, or destroying specific property without the permission of the owner. The right to exclude thus achieved the first great objective of any social order: the separation of me from thee, and indeed from everyone else. Its great virtue is that it is *scalable*. The content of the right, or knowledge of what it entails, is independent of the number of people in the group. The rule of uniform forbearance works equally well in small communities and large metropolises. Private property, however, would be a feeble social institution if it covered only the right to exclude. Literally understood, that right would not guarantee the owner his own use of the land or things from which others were excluded. The standard bundle of property rights in particular resources therefore has never been so impoverished as to stop with exclusion. Everywhere, ownership also includes rights to use, transform, develop, consume, or dispose of property. This "bundle" of rights should not be derided as some arbitrary assemblage of the so-called incidents of ownership. Indeed the Supreme Court has repeatedly endorsed (but not fully honored) this account of private property in its takings cases, because no other definition will do.

This historical account contains a deep functional unity that holds true to the present day. To see why, consider how the world of private ownership would look if any one of these rights were removed from the bundle. A right to enter but not to use would be of no value to the owner, while conferring no value to anyone else. Nor would there be any way to cure the defect, for there would be no identifiable person from whom the supposed owner could obtain the rights to use, develop, and consume. So including all of these rights in the bundle from the outset not only accords with standard usage but also produces gains to one person. Indeed, far from imposing losses on anyone else, it increases everyone's welfare by opening up opportunities for trade.

That's where the rights of disposition come in. First, let's be clear as to the comprehensive nature of this term. It covers the outright sale or gift of property, during life or at death, from one person to another. In these cases, the new owner just steps into the shoes of the prior owner, and enjoys the same rights against the rest of the world. But the true genius of property rights is how they facilitate more complex forms of both joint and divided control of resources, both of which allow for specialization and cooperation between persons. The present owner may contribute his land to a partnership where his resources are pooled with those of others. That partnership could lease property for a term of years instead of selling it. Or they could mortgage it, as security for a loan. Alternatively, an owner may retain the right to use the land for life, by giving his or her children a right to the land at his or her death.

Nor need all the rights in property relate to the single parcel of land. The complex law of servitudes allows people to create both easements and restrictive covenants over the lands of other people. An easement allows, for example, one person to walk across the land of another, or drive his cattle to the riverfront. A restrictive covenant arises when an owner gives up his ordinary rights of development and use, by agreeing, for example, not to use his property for a brewery, or not to build a structure more than 30 feet high or within 10 feet of the property line.

Once the process of disposition gets going, it has no natural end, for any property rights obtained in one transaction can be resold or repackaged in the next. Partners could lease property subject to a mortgage and a restrictive covenant, but benefited by an easement. The difficult problems with ownership lie in keeping track of these multiple interests, which requires a central facility for the recording of deeds for all to examine before they transact. This conscious form of state regulation provides stability for relations between trading partners. Simultaneously, it supplies notice to the rest of the world as to who must maintain the property, and who is presently in the position to sell, mortgage, or lease it. In so doing, the recording system increases gains from trade by blocking double-dealing. The entire system of property rights creates huge opportunities for gains from trade that could not be realized if ownership rights were confined to exclusion, possession, use, consumption, and development.

In sum, each element of the property picture has its own function: exclusion separates individuals and helps maintain peace and good order; use and development allow for individuals to gain sustenance and comfort; and disposition allows for people to combine their efforts in ways that take advantage of the division of labor for their mutual advantage. The historical rules, therefore, have a real substantive unity that helps explain why earlier writers concluded that the whole system conformed to a natural reason that spanned the globe.

PRIVATE PROPERTY: THE DOWNSIDE

If the upside to private property is evident, so, on refection, is its downside. Let us look now at the three central features of property—exclusion, use, and disposition—in a more skeptical frame of mind.

Rights of exclusion work well when those excluded have other choices. Thus the right to exclude allows for the emergence of a competitive market for home sales. But exclusion turns more ominous when the property owner is the only game in town. That situation can arise in so-called cases of private necessity, where, for example, a person stranded at sea can save himself and his ship from imminent peril only by clambering to safety on someone else's dock. The general solution: the party in peril can enter the dock as of right (such that the owner is at that moment not allowed to exclude him) so long as he pays rent for using the dock plus compensation for any harm caused. Necessities are not solely limited to these circumstances but can also arise whenever a property owner is the sole supplier of some critical good or service. When customers have access to only a single port, inn, or railroad, the common law traditionally obligated the facility owners to serve all members of the public at reasonable and nondiscriminatory rates. That rule avoided two extremes: the danger that the owner would hold out for huge sums of money, and the danger that low rates would make it impossible for the owner to recover the costs of his investments, plus a reasonable profit. Modern rate regulation has its origins in these historical rules.

In most cases, however, it is efficient to assign the single owner exclusive use rights for each piece of property. But exclusive use is not unlimited use of property. Every legal system has to decide how to limit one person's use of his rights in order to protect his neighbor's. These obligations must be strictly reciprocal, so that any duties imposed on A for the benefit of his neighbors are likewise imposed on each neighbor for the benefit of A. The challenge is to create a common regime that will maximize the value of the individual holdings, which happens only when restrictions on use cost each owner less than the benefits they afford his neighbors.

Searching for this elusive "average reciprocity of advantage" generates some easy results. It makes sense for each owner not to enter the land of his neighbor without permission, or to build structures that overhang his neighbor's land, or to shoot missiles over the land of another. Put the restrictions on all together, and as an empirical matter, each person will gain more from these restrictions imposed on others than he will suffer when like restrictions are imposed on him. The legal regime thus treats direct entry as a trespass that has to be justified or excused, as for example by the need to rescue a stranger or abate a nuisance. It applies the same view toward ordinary nuisance, which occurs when the activities of one person generate noise, pollution, dust, or odors that disturb others in the quiet enjoyment of their land. In general, the common law protects each owner against nuisances by twin remedies: damages for past violations and an injunction against future ones.

This initial judgment is not categorical, without regard to the size or extent of the nuisance. Thus, the principle of reciprocity routinely holds that no individual can protest the routine low-level sounds and smells of his neighbor. Now the order of advantage is reversed, in that the large benefits of these common uses to the owner outweigh the trivial costs to others—at least until the music that is tolerable during the day keeps neighbors awake at night. Of course, there is no one "right" balance: busy neighborhoods tolerate higher levels of disruption than residential ones, under the so-called locality rule. Cases can become still more vexed, for example, if the injured plaintiff has "come to the nuisance" by building his house next to a noisy factory.

In general, noninvasive activities that reduce the value of a neighbor's property are not nuisances. Thus it is lawful to build a tall structure on one's own land that blocks the light and air of a neighbor. The gains from more intensive utilization outstrip the inconvenience from lost views. And there is danger that this rule will encourage people to build early in order to block out a neighbor. Nor has the common law ever used the law of nuisance to prevent one person from opening a business in competition with a neighbor. Nonetheless, certain forms of *non*invasive conduct, such as digging out land to the boundary line to cause collapse of a neighbor's land, are treated as nuisances, because of a switch in the anticipated ratio of benefit to burden. A related example is the so-called support estate, which requires the owner of mineral rights to take out his ore in ways that do not cause the surface to collapse. In addition, some states adopt rules that make it unlawful to erect "spite" fences (but never houses), which are built with malice to block a neighbor's light or air. All of these rules have explicit constitutional parallels.

In dealing with this complex body of law that regulates boundary disputes, the central effort of matching land use with land restrictions is intended to maximize the portfolio value of rights attached to each plot of land. Obviously in some situations, these off-the-rack rules will not work. In these settings, neighboring landowners may correct any imbalance by entering into private agreements that are memorialized in various restrictions. These restrictions are said to "run" with the land, that is, to apply not only to the current owners, but to all people who acquire property through them in subsequent transactions. The basic principle is that parties by agreement can reverse the common-law rules, by creating easements to legalize nuisances, or imposing restrictive covenants to prohibit otherwise lawful uses. Occasionally, these easements and covenants are purchased in separate transactions. More often, a developer of a subdivision or condominiums imposes these easements and covenants, without cash transfers, pursuant to a common plan prior to the initial sale.

Disposition

A similar analysis applies to the rights of disposition, which may break down in one of two ways. Even ordinary contracts for sale can fail if the property is incorrectly described or if one party uses duress, fraud, or concealment to take advantage of another. Nor does the right to transfer property from A to B justify transfers that generate harmful consequences to third persons. A may not sell weapons to help B kill or maim C. The class of suspect contracts also includes, more controversially, collusive deals between two or more individuals to raise prices or reduce output. In essence, this prohibition is meant to prevent two or more persons from acting in concert to take the dominant position of a common carrier, by eliminating competition between themselves. The analysis is more complicated, since many business agreements have mixed consequences, because they create monopoly power on the one hand and enhance economic efficiency on the other. The proper response may be to ban the combination or merger, or to allow it to go forward subject to limitations on rates. But however difficult it is to combat collusion, one point remains clear: the state should never use force to restrict competition in the open market.

FROM PRIVATE PROPERTY TO THE
SOCIAL CONTRACT

The common-law evolution of property rights I have sketched here has been replicated in other societies with vastly different social traditions. To be sure, all legal systems differ in how they implement these rights. For example, the choice of formalities used to execute and record land transfers may differ from one society to the next. One society may use formal ceremonies, while the second uses a simple deed. Similarly, the law of nuisance varies on fine points across nations, even between different states of the United States. But we must not overestimate the extent of the variation in legal rules across social systems. So long as societies must find ways both to keep people apart and to bring them together, societies will gravitate to analogous rules for the acquisition, protection, and disposition of property. Indeed, borrowing between legal systems is common, precisely because each culture is receptive to seeds from all the others, given that all laws of physics are invariant across cultures. The consistency, regularity, and functionality across legal systems should not be underestimated. Those instructive parallels supply the foundation for a durable constitutional order that can survive the fads and fancies of the moment.

Yet if these rules contain the raw stuff needed to maintain a consistent legal order, why and how do they take hold? The usual answer from the British and American tradition is through social contract theory. In one sense, this term is an oxymoron. All individuals living in some given territory cannot enter into any complex set of reciprocal agreements whereby all agree to support a state by whose laws they agree to be bound, any more than they can actually agree to respect the liberty and property of others. No one could assemble everyone, including those not yet born, at a single time and place. And even for those people who could come together, nothing prevents some individuals from holding out for a better deal than the rest. Nor is it plausible to posit any implied consent by individuals who have had no contact with each other. Notwithstanding these obvious difficulties, how did social contract theory come to exert a tenacious hold on John Locke and his followers? The account of property relations I have outlined here (along with analogous conceptions of personal liberty) at most sets out the desirable rules of the game. But these rules are not self-enforcing. In a world devoid of government, each person has to execute the laws on his own behalf against others who violate them. It would be a mistake to treat private enforcement as wholly worthless in the face of the powerful forces of individual self-interest. In most communities, rules against the use of force and in favor of voluntary exchange have enough traction to discourage many would-be wrongdoers, even in the absence of any centralized system of enforcement. Most individuals are not the relentlessly selfish human beings postulated by Thomas Hobbes, and are usually guided by deep moral intuitions they find it difficult to ignore or articulate. Furthermore, living in families and clans has habituated most people to some level of social cooperation. As David Hume put it, personal self-interest is constrained by a "confined generosity," which helps lay the foundations for a political order.

Even so, self-enforcement leaves much to be desired, owing to the bias all individuals have in their own favor. The centripetal forces are likely to rip a society apart, unless a single sovereign enjoys a monopoly of force that provides a known and impartial system of justice to protect the rights of all people to, as it is said, life, liberty, and property. On this view, the state is not an arbitrary institution imposed from above that may, with the stroke of a pen, adopt whatever conceptions of liberty and property it chooses.

Rather, the object of the state is to preserve as much of the basic system of liberty and property as is consistent with the maintenance of peace and social order.

Social contract theory thus takes on two overlapping roles. The first offers a descriptive account of the transition from a state of nature (or clans and tribes) to the modern political state. The second offers a normative account of how that transition might be justified. Any descriptive account is highly imperfect, because much social organization had its root in conquest and bloodshed. But by the same token, some primitive forms of cooperation surely aided the move toward territorial government. The normative account, however, has far greater appeal because it indicates how a well-ordered society could have emerged from the state of nature.

How then does social contract theory help any group of individuals achieve its normative objective? The answer lies, I think, in looking at the two words separately, and then combining their meaning. Start with the term "contract": contracts are ubiquitous in all legal systems because they supply the only known means for the voluntary exchange of goods and services. And why do we care about that? Because each voluntary exchange increases the satisfaction of all parties to it. Such exchanges therefore result in the presumptive social improvement of win–win transactions. We know right away that two people who voluntarily contract are both better off than before. But what about the consequences to third parties? Some contracts, such as contracts to use force or restrain trade, may hurt third parties. But in most instances, contracts are clearly positive. Increased wealth for the contracting parties routinely spells increased opportunities for third persons. The global situation is thus win–win for both parties and strangers.

The law of contract thus sets this aspiration for all social arrangements: an across-the-board improvement of all individuals who are both benefited and bound by a set of political arrangements. Using the term "social" marks a subtle concession that individual consent is not the means to a desired end. The term "social" indicates that the state is allowed to use force to achieve the win–win objective of voluntary agreements. Clearly that goal is dashed if the sovereign uses the monopoly of power to enrich himself. Sound government requires each person to forfeit some fraction of his liberty and property to supply the state with the authority and resources needed to enforce prior entitlements to liberty and property. This social contract seeks to mimic the voluntary agreement the multiple parties would make with each other if only they could. Each person should gain from the creation of a political order more personal satisfaction (or "utility") than he attached to the liberty and property that he has contributed to the mix. If that condition is satisfied, then state power is justified by the benefits government supplies in return—benefits that could not be achieved by voluntary agreement, owing to the huge transactional barriers in the state of nature.

But what kinds of arrangements satisfy this objective? Thomas Hobbes insisted that all individuals in a state of nature were so wretched that they would take any bone thrown in their direction by a despotic sovereign who offered peace. But the rejoinder asks, why stop at half measures? Even though tyranny is better than anarchy, constitutional governance could be better than both. Private organizations rely on the board of directors to discipline the chief executive officer, and give the shareholders limited rights to control both. The political analogy is the separation of legislative and executive powers to curb the abuses of excessive concentration of power.

Yet how does the legislature gain its power to pass laws and collect taxes? An instructive ambiguity in the logic of John Locke helps explain why the just compensation language makes its way into the Fifth Amendment. Locke's problem was to legitimate taxation. His answer seizes on the notion of consent drawn from social contract theory. But his fatal equivocation reveals the breakdown of consent-based theories of political authority. Thus sometimes Locke writes that taxation requires the individual consent of *each* person. But he does not explain how he overcomes the same holdout risks that play havoc with the consensual explanations for the origin of property in the state of nature. So Locke switches gears and treats taxation as a matter of legislative consent by majority vote, which invites differential taxation that taxes one group of citizens to support another. The consent language thus exhausts itself. In one version, consent leads to institutional paralysis; in the other, it leads to expropriation.

Locke rejected both extremes in favor of a view that accepts taxes that are proportionate to the benefit each individual receives from government services. This theme of proportionate taxation, which runs through all theorists of limited government, including Adam Smith and Friedrich Hayek, rests on a clear conception of the uses of government coercion. This conception is best represented by a simple diagram of two concentric pies divided into uneven slices, with a common center. (See opposite page.)

The inner pie represents the value individuals attach to their liberty and property in the state of nature. The slices are drawn in uneven sizes to reflect the natural differences in their holdings. Variation in talents and ability is an inescapable feature of biological and social life. The traditional social contract theory of government, unlike modern egalitarian theories, aims only to control aggression and other forms of misbehavior. It does *not* seek to even out bad luck in natural endowments or social connections through massive transfer payments. Once the size of those slices is settled, the objective of taxation is to move proportionately all individuals to a higher level of satisfaction. The theory thus does not disturb the relative ranking of persons, but

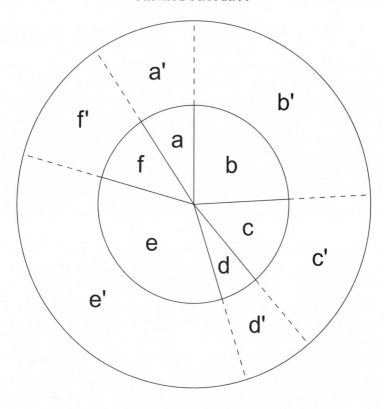

equalizes the rate of return on each person's forced contribution to the government. Adam Smith analogized the distributions of tax benefits and burdens of taxation to those in a well-run partnership. In effect, the law adopts a *nondiscrimination* principle that seeks to bridge the gap between individual and unanimous consent. The basic deal runs as follows. The majority gets to choose the level of taxation, but members of the winning coalition pay the same taxes as members of the minority. Obviously, this principle cannot eliminate all forms of social conflict, since different people make different estimates of the worth of any government program that impacts them all. For those collective decisions, politics is the only way people can work through their differences. Even with this important caveat, the following basic pattern emerges for social cooperation. The state through coercive action takes property from all people. The nondiscrimination rule is the best tool for ensuring that each person receives just compensation in the form of greater peace and security shared by all. The more limited the scope of government, the more likely it is that the nondiscrimination principle will be able to function to prevent factional strife, for interpersonal conflicts are less likely to surface about the need to preserve law and order than they are, for example, on the proper form of education, where clashes between religious and secular views are likely to be great. The coercive arrangements are intended to duplicate the outcomes of Smith's well-ordered partnership—mutual gains for all.

This approach toward taxation does not single out any individual for special treatment. The tax is levied in dollars, and each person figures out which assets to use in order to pay the bill. In some cases, however, the government has to take specific property at a given location for a road or a fort, and in these circumstances the lockstep treatment of citizens is no longer preserved. The problem is thus addressed by the power of eminent domain. For these specific assets, taxes from general revenues are used to pay the owner just compensation for the property taken, which is then devoted to public use. The use of compensation thus prevents any single individual or small group from being "singled out" for special adverse treatment, for the cash paid is meant to be a perfect equivalent of the property surrendered.

The political theory then points to a general approach regarding the use of state power for the provision of public goods and services. Every forced transaction, whether by taxation or eminent domain, should yield proportionate gains to all individuals. The simple fact that all individuals gain ensures that each government project generates what is called, after the Italian economist Vilfredo Pareto, a Pareto improvement—government action leaves at least one person better off and no one worse off than before. Indeed, the proportionate gain requirement, so often defended on intuitive grounds of fairness, imposes an even more exacting condition, namely, that government coercion give each individual an equal return on his or her contribution to society, to the extent that human institutions can make this happen.

Forcing the government to supply proportionate gains necessarily shrinks the level of factional intrigue. Let there be a society of ten persons, each of whom starts with 100 units; now imagine a social improvement, such as a road through a town, that generates a gain of 500 units for all. Without proportionality, each person would jockey to get as much of that 500-unit gain for himself. Anyone is allowed to do just that, so long as he leaves everyone else at the 100-unit level or above. By our earlier definition, that skewed result generates a Pareto improvement even if one citizen garners the entire 500 units in gain, because no one else is made worse off. But any willingness to tolerate these skewed distributions of gain invites prolonged political battles over the division of this surplus, as each person fights to garner as much of the social surplus as he can. Those struggles cost a lot of time and money to wage, generating backstabbing and conflict along the way. The combined effect of these political maneuvers is to eliminate much of the 500 units in gain that the social project originally promised. The proration requirement offers an effective way to counter that risk, for it generates a unique allocation of that 500 units—fifty per person—that prevents their dissipation through costly factional intrigue.

In fact, this simple diagram becomes the paradigm for all government projects, no matter whether their initial incidence is equal across all individuals, as in taxation, or differs across individuals, as with the taking of specific property. It should now be clear why the inclusion of the takings clause in the Constitution resonates so strongly with individuals who were schooled in the classical liberal tradition. It represents a twelve-word distillation of social contract political theory. Theory, however, is one thing. Its application to a huge range of social settings is quite another. And that is in large measure the task of constitutional interpretation, to which I next turn.

CHAPTER TWO

. . .

The Generative Power of
Constitutional Interpretation

WITHOUT DOUBT, the *second* most important question in American constitutional law deals with interpretation: what are the appropriate ways to read and understand particular provisions of the Constitution that govern the actions of all branches of government (the judiciary included)? Why is this only the second most important question? Because the most important question of constitutional theory focuses on judicial review, namely the question of whether the courts, at either the federal or the state level, may invoke the Constitution to strike down legislation that meets all the formal requirements needed to make the law. The broad scope of judicial review raises the stakes on all interpretive issues, for once it is decided that the courts—and ultimately the Supreme Court—have the power to invalidate legislation that meets all the formal criteria for law, then courts may override even considered decisions of the political branches of government. That power may be invoked not only when lawmakers act in wild and irresponsible ways but also when their sober judgment reflects the considered sentiments of the clear majority of political actors and ordinary citizens.

JUDICIAL REVIEW

Judicial review has almost no pedigree in political theory prior to the adoption of our Constitution, for the system of separation of power in England featured the Crown and the two houses of Parliament. To be sure, the English courts often gave a narrow reading to parliamentary enactments that flouted fundamental principles of natural justice. But unlike the modern principle of judicial review, the English practice did not allow courts to invalidate statutes whose meaning, however unjust, was too clear to admit of doubt. Nor did it rest on the existence of a written constitution.

Judicial review in the American context goes far beyond the earlier English practice, for it gives courts the power to invalidate statutes as inconsistent with the commands of a higher law, the Constitution. The justifications for this antidemocratic practice are still contested to this day, and it is not possible here to examine the theoretical or textual arguments on both sides of this arcane debate. But now that judicial review is entrenched in American law, its awesome reach underscores the imperative need for courts to develop principled guidelines for dealing with the multiple forms of government action, including taxation and regulation. No student of political institutions believes that virtue is lodged in one branch of political power and vice in another. The Constitution divided power in order to tame it. The first cut was the division between federal and state powers. The second, at the federal level, introduced a system that separated power among the legislative, executive, and judicial branches, with a host of checks and balances among them. The Constitution divided the federal powers in this way because its drafters wanted a structure that had the best chance of proving resistant to misbehavior from every quarter. Without knowing what issues would prove controversial in the future, or the personalities of future political leaders, the founders hedged their bets by parceling out power in many hands, hoping for the best. Once judicial review became established, courts faced a pressing need to develop a coherent and persuasive theory of interpretation. Without sound rules of interpretation, judicial review could upset the original balance of power. But how?

One way to avoid usurping legislative and executive powers is for all courts to defer routinely to them. This view requires courts to presume that all statutes are constitutional. Courts thus strike down only those few statutes that manifest a flagrant disregard for the Constitution. But the vice of such deference is the flip side of its virtue. Our constitutional heritage showed no special fondness for popular democracy that operated by an unvarnished principle of majority rule. The founders adopted complex institutional arrangements to keep transient majorities from seizing government power for long-term partisan advantage. In the common usage of the time, *democracy* was not a term of praise but referred to a deviant form of a republic, which featured indirect elections and other checks on popular control. That republican theory is reflected in the various restrictions on simple majorities that the Constitution contains. No theory of judicial deference could allow the election of a thirty-year-old president, when the Constitution sets an age minimum of thirty-five years. Nor does it allow Congress to override a presidential veto by a 60 percent vote in each house, when the Constitution sets a two-thirds requirement in both houses. These fixed numerical standards are too clear to allow for interpretive disputes.

Text and Context

Unfortunately, the clarity found in these procedural and voting rules is not mirrored in the takings clause or in the First Amendment's guarantee of freedom of speech, or in the relationship between the free exercise of religion, which is protected, and the establishment of religion (as either the creation of a state church or a set of religious preferences), which is forbidden. Yet, the practice of judicial review, which allows the courts to invalidate otherwise valid laws, also applies to these provisions, even though they leave huge areas to judicial interpretation. Courts might adopt a stance of extreme deference to political actors, but only by gutting expansive constitutional protections in ways that are not faithful to our constitutional tradition of limited government. The text of the takings clause (which before the passage of the Fourteenth Amendment in 1868 applied only to the actions of the federal government), for example, does not read "Nor shall private property be taken for public use, without just compensation, except when Congress and/or the President have dreamed up some fanciful reason to justify their actions." Nor does the clause bless all good faith efforts of Congress to comply with its requirements. Rather, the provision is written in the categorical form typical of all constitutional guarantees, so what really matters is whether Congress and the executive in fact meet the constitutional norm. At the minimum, it is a judicial question of whether private property has been taken, whether that taking was for public use, and whether just compensation was supplied. The entire enterprise makes sense because it takes seriously the risk that actions of the political branches may exceed their limited constitutional powers. Human institutions must learn to live with inevitable uncertainty. Like any other social practice, therefore, judicial review has to take into account two forms of error: (1) striking down legislation and blocking executive action that is constitutional or (2) upholding government action that violates constitutional norms.

The endless debates over judicial activism and judicial passivity do little to resolve general interpretive problems or to decide individual cases. So put aside any broad presumptions. Whether courts deal with the structural provisions of the Constitution (that is, those that set out the respective roles for the various branches of the federal government) or with specific guarantees of individual rights, the acid test is the same: have courts read constitutional terms in accord with their ordinary usage at the time of their adoption, as elucidated—and here is the rub—by traditional principles of interpretation.

One component of the interpretive enterprise is to explicate the four key terms of the takings clause. What do we mean by "private property"? How is it "taken"? What is "just compensation"? And what is a taking "for public use"? But it would be a grievous error to assume that these textual questions, critical as they are to the overall enterprise, constitute the entire picture. In fact, they require supplementation by two key *non*textual principles of interpretation that are wholly consistent with the rule of law, and that have always been an integral part of a uniform interpretive tradition since the days of the Bible. For ease of exposition, let us refer to these principles as the anticircumvention principle and the justification principle. Taken together, these principles address the inevitable dangers of under- and over-inclusion in the articulation of any general substantive command, both in constitutional and everyday disputes.

Anticircumvention

Two historical examples illustrate the interaction between text and structure. A biblical commandment says quite simply "Thou shalt not kill." An analogous provision of Roman law, called the Lex Aquilia, says that no person shall kill unlawfully the slave or herd animal owned by another person. Both provisions garner general approbation, for no one defends the proposition that allows people to kill with impunity. The moment the prohibition is in place, however, we can expect to see self-interested people work to circumvent its literal language in ways that undermine its broad purpose of preserving human life from the machinations of others. Thus, everyone has to agree that I violate the commandment by stabbing you with a knife or forcing poison down your throat. But now suppose that I cleverly conceal a trap on your front walkway with blades at the bottom, or I put arsenic in your pepper soup. You are killed when you fall into the trap or sip the soup. Can I deny responsibility for your death by claiming that the real cause of death was your false step or soup sipping?

Of course your action complicates the analysis, but that should not allow me to escape liability. We would have a harder problem if you went ahead knowing of the deadly trap or the poisoned soup. But concealment matters: so long as your actions were taken in ignorance of the danger, *every* legal system holds me responsible for your death. Setting a trap or furnishing poison is treated as killing. Nor would the result differ if I held a gun to your head and forced you to jump into the trap or eat the soup. But if there is neither deception nor coercion, then, in an account that goes back at least to Aristotle, the anticircumvention principle no longer applies. You are the author of your own doom.

This anticircumvention rule has its precise analogue to all forms of government coercion and deception. Thus the state cannot force you to deed your house over at a point of the knife. Nor can the state first blow up your house and then pay only for the rubble. Nor can it threaten to seize your house if you do not agree to contribute half of its value in cash to the public treasury. Nonetheless, there are limits. This ancient interpretive strategy does not block an individual from donating property to the government of his own free will. The anticircumvention principle, when fleshed out by the twin libertarian prohibitions against coercion and concealment, stops government abuse, without imposing impossible fetters on government action.

Justification

If the anticircumvention principle expands the scope of the takings clause, the justification principle narrows it. This principle allows the government to explain why actions that are prima facie wrong are in fact proper. At the outset, it is useful to give some sense of how the terms "prima facie" and "justification" are used. The Latin "prima facie" means literally "at first look," and "justification" (which derives from the Latin "ius," *right* or *law*) refers to circumstances that make right—not merely excuse—any action that is prima facie wrong.

Why should we trouble ourselves about justifications in an analysis of the takings clause that does not mention them at all? Once again, the analogies drawn from the private law prove decisive. One person may use force to take, without compensation, a knife from his assailant. Make this modest concession, and you are off to the races. May he use deadly force to protect his $2 fountain pen? If there is some lesser means of force available? If the threatened attack might not take place? If the attacker labors under serious disability? Volumes have been written about excessive force, proportionate force, and mistaken force. Once self-defense is read into a text that makes no reference to it, then much hard work is required to distinguish between a *killing*, which may be justified, and *murder*, for which by definition no justification is possible. Virtually all texts necessarily give rise to similar non-textual questions.

The same difficulties arise with regard to potential harms to land. If your neighbor creates a nuisance on his own property, can you enter his land to abate the nuisance immediately, or must you wait until the fumes or other discharges reach your own property, or damage your plants or wildlife? Can you destroy his offending structures to prevent a repetition of the harm? Does it make a difference if you built your garden before he built his factory, instead of the other way around? Does this difference count in cases of potentially deadly emissions? Can you treat an ugly house as a nuisance, even if it emits no noises or smells?

These justifications make their way into constitutional law under the heading of the *police power*—a sprawling topic that asks what kinds of justifications, such as nuisance prevention, allow the state to limit the use of private property *without paying compensation*. The term "police power" appears nowhere in the Constitution, but it is pervasive in constitutional analysis. All the standard nineteenth-century treatises on constitutional law included the term "police power" in their title. Under the classical definitions, the police power covers cases where the state limits the use of property to protect the "health, safety, general welfare, and morals of the community." A clear understanding comes from taking the phrase more literally. Has your neighbor done something that makes it proper for you to call in the police for protection against various types of wrongs, of which harms to person and property are most common? In connection with the takings clause, most disputes center on entries and nuisances to land. You may be protected in your use of private property, but you cannot use it to spew filth that renders your neighbor's land worthless. Every legal system has to build some antinuisance exception to the permissible uses of private property, only to sort out its qualifications thereafter through rules every bit as complex as those regulating self-defense or defense of property.

An Instructive Synergy

The difficulties in working with these two interpretive principles are compounded by their joint operation, which pulls in opposite directions. The broad constitutional protections afforded private property, speech, and religion should never be interpreted as absolutes. Rather, singling these interests out for constitutional protection marks only the opening salvo in an extended inquiry that must incorporate both the anticircumvention and justification principles. Believe in free speech, and you have to decide whether its protection covers plays, flag burning, and the Internet. But no matter how broadly construed, freedom of speech does not constitutionally protect people who extort, bribe, defame, or deceive. Short texts necessarily and properly require extensive explication.

THE UNITY OF TAKINGS LAW

This brief analysis of general interpretive principles now puts us in a position to construe the takings clause in relation to the full range of government actions. First, we should ask, what does it mean to take private property? The answer to this question reveals the close connection between the private law principles developed in chapter 1 and the proper constitutional approach. The analysis of the statement "A has taken the private property of B" carries the same meaning whether A is a private person or the state. Modern commentators routinely reject the equivalence between the common-law and constitutional conceptions of takings. They insist, generally, that property rights are not prior to the state, but come only from collective political decisions. More concretely, they argue that the takings clause gives the owner of private property strong protections against being dispossessed of his property in so-called physical takings cases, but gives the owner only weak protection against state regulation of the use or disposition of property, in so-called regulatory takings cases.

Under current law, the distinction between physical and regulatory takings has two important consequences. First, courts give a high, or "strict," level of scrutiny to physical takings. The potential justifications that allow these takings without compensation are limited, which is as it should be. In addition, the equivalence between public and private law means that in all cases the amount of compensation is determined by what the owner loses, not what he retains. Start with land worth $10,000. If the state takes three-fourths of the land such that the value of the residue is $2,500, then the proper level of compensation is $7,500, leaving the owner with the same wealth that he had before the government action. But instead suppose that the state leaves the owner in possession of the land, but imposes fresh restrictions on its use—size, height, and setback restrictions, for example—that reduce its value by 75 percent. For these so-called regulatory takings, courts today no longer ask how much diminution in value the restriction on property rights caused. Rather they ask whether any "viable economic use" of the property remains. If so, then the landowner receives no compensation, no matter how much is lost. In the above example, the owner absorbs the full $7,500 in loss.

This modern approach to regulatory takings necessarily rejects in the constitutional realm the private law view that private property embraces the right to exclude, use, develop, and dispose of property. This artificial separation of constitutional from common-law meaning also undermines the entire system of private legal arrangements of the common law (which, as we have seen, maximize the joint value of all property owners). Thus, suppose that a group of neighbors wants to turn a vacant lot into a public park. They are of course free to raise funds to acquire the land at market price. So long as the park is meant for public use, they can urge the municipal government to appropriate tax dollars and condemn the land at market price. But they should not be able to ask the city council to designate this property as public without any compensation at all.

The power to designate should be no greater when the neighbors abandon their efforts to convert the vacant lot into a public park but instead only seek to prevent owners from building on it in ways that block their view. Rather, the neighbors are entitled to band together and offer the owner a sum of money to accept restrictions that prevent or limit construction by the owner or his successors in title. (Alternatively, they could purchase the land outright from the owner and then resell it for less, subject to whatever restrictions they desire.) So constrained, the neighbors compare their benefits with the owner's costs every step of the way. But why should some owners, who must pay a market rate to acquire a covenant privately, be able to obtain it *for free* by prevailing on the legislature to impose the identical restrictions on another owner for their benefit? It takes no political genius to realize that the neighbors will flock to the city council to obtain the desired restrictions without payment. If the common-law rights are efficient, then this brave new world of weak entitlements must be less so, as the entire structure of private property rights becomes undermined in countless zoning hearings that force some landowners to defend ordinary common-law building rights that their neighbors covet. Money that would otherwise be transferred from buyer to seller now gets wasted in political intrigue. The common-law rules allow owners *not* to develop land without loss of rights. The new zoning system gives the strong incentive to build prematurely solely to protect development and use rights from political risk.

One defense of this broad state power insists that the government should not have to compensate owners for the "mere" diminution in property values attributable solely to state action. They analogize the losses in value from regulation to those attributable to losses from private competition. But the parallel fails. Private owners do not have to provide compensation when their competitive activities reduce the value of nearby land. But the right to compete does not allow them to use force to restrict their neighbor's land use as of right outside the confines of the common law of nuisance. Good reason supports that distinction. Competition advances overall wealth. Restriction of competition by private fiat destroys that wealth by distorting private behavior.

The distinction between competition and restriction survives when the state enters the picture. The government acts solely as an agent for the citizens it benefits when it restricts the land use of others. The state could not impose those restrictions at all if they did not satisfy the public use requirement. But even when they do, the resultant harm from land use regulation does not stem from the operation of competitive forces. That harm is not a mere diminution in value. It is a diminution in value consequent on the loss of a recognized property right for which compensation is owed.

The crucial modern constitutional distinction between physical and regulatory takings thus rests on intellectual quicksand. To see the intuition, imagine that the bundle of rights in a piece of land—in space, over time, and against neighbors—is a salami. Any slice of that salami is still salami, so that the state has to pay for each slice of the salami it cuts for itself, no matter how thin. The more it takes, the more it pays. How it slices or dices the salami may affect how much compensation is owed, but never defeats the basic obligation. Everyone concedes that the takings clause is an empty letter if it does not require compensation when the government takes an entire plot of land for its own use. The result holds if it takes only half the land, or if it occupies the entire land for a fixed number of years, or if it enters the land only after a certain number of years has passed. The result does not change if the government only claims an easement over land, without throwing its owner off entirely. Nor does the government escape liability by subjecting a single owner to a restrictive covenant that prevents him from building on all or some of his land, forever or for any definite period of time. Each of these actions takes some fraction of the basic rights in land. It would be odd if the takings clause were read to hold "Nor shall private property be taken for public use, without just compensation, but bits and pieces of it can always be taken for free, so long as some shred remains with the original owner." Rather, the evident sense of the clause is that private property shall not be taken, *either in whole or in part*, for public use, without just compensation. Which parts are taken is determined by the common law of property. The compensation is determined by the loss in value. The situation is perfectly continuous. There is no troublesome gap between those forms of takings that are too slight to merit compensation and those that are substantial enough to require it. The maxim—the more you take, the more you pay—gives the right incentives for responsible social action. The state will take the land, or some fractional interest in it, only if it can generate public benefits higher than the private costs it imposes.

Regulation frequently differs from actions directed to a single property owner, in that it covers many owners at once. For example, "spot zoning" ordinances carve out zones with only one or very few property owners. But these differences between spot and comprehensive ordinances are only relevant to the question of how much compensation is owed. They are irrelevant to whether property has been taken. Thus, assume that a land use restriction is placed on the land of two persons instead of one. We now have two takings, each of which should be presumptively compensated for the value lost. Increase the number of parties subjected to the ordinance, and the answer remains the same: the greater the number of people from whom you take, the greater the number of people you have to compensate. In physical takings cases, it is commonly recognized that the duty to compensate remains regardless of the number of persons whose property is taken. The same logic applies to land use restrictions. In both cases, there is no categorical distinction between "spot" and "comprehensive" government actions. Both generate the same presumptive obligation to compensate. Politicians no longer have an incentive to shape their restrictions to avoid the obligations to compensate.

This analysis denies that there is any plausible dividing line between compensable occupations and noncompensable regulations. Rather, two continuous transformations link these together. First we *reduce* the fraction of land taken from each person: we now have only a bit of salami from each. Second, we *expand* the number of persons who are subject to the regulation. Neither move undercuts the presumptive obligation to compensate. All government action that takes property rights constitutes a taking regardless of the nature or amount of rights taken from any one person, and regardless of the number of persons subject to the government action.

This comprehensive view of what counts as a taking has important consequences not only for government action, but also for private transactions in land. So long as property receives this comprehensive form of protection, ordinary private transactions need not be shaped to protect a property owner against state regulation. Hence, if regulated individuals are entitled to compensation only if their interests are wiped out, then they will fragment their property interests to increase the odds of getting compensation, by selling off air rights that it might otherwise be more efficient to retain. There is no good reason to force private parties to enter into unnecessary transactions in order to secure greater protection of their rights, or, conversely, to force them to refrain from making sensible divisions of property rights that increase their takings exposure. The gamesmanship will cease so long as the private division and combination of property rights only determine *who* receives compensation, and not *whether* any compensation is owed. Private parties will engage in those transactions that maximize value whether or not the state intervenes. Any system that offers only discontinuous protection of property rights encourages all parties to play games up and down the line.

This conceptual framework is often attacked as incomplete. Thus far, it has not taken into account the spillovers, both positive and negative, between neighbors. But the analysis of takings law does not stop with the question "When is property taken?" Three other questions—regarding public use, police power, and just compensation—remain. The matter of spillovers is, in fact, fully addressed with police power and just compensation. First, the state can regulate to prevent nuisances. Second, the role of just compensation becomes greater with the two variables just mentioned: the extent of the property interest taken and the number of people subject to the regulation. As the regulation takes smaller interests in property from a larger number of landowners, the odds increase that the network of restrictions supplies *implicit in-kind compensation* to each regulated party. The compensation is implicit because it is not separately provided by a separate government transfer. It is in-kind because it comes in the form of a restriction on the property rights of others. You benefit because I cannot build above a certain height, and I benefit because you are subject to the same restriction. The benefits are thus parallel and reciprocal. Private developers use just this strategy when homeowners in subdivisions and condominiums are subject to extensive land use restrictions. But implicit in-kind compensation is not found in all extensive schemes, many of which are heavily skewed.

Public officials have very different incentives from private developers. The former respond to factional politics. The latter impose restrictions solely to increase the overall value of the project, which in turn increases their net profit on sale. If you don't like the rules, don't buy into the project. But zoning is different: individual landowners cannot protect themselves from majority will by refusing to buy in. Some zoning schemes increase the value of all regulated lands. But many consciously regulate some landowners to benefit others located nearby. It is thus necessary to look at the impact of comprehensive schemes person by person, without assumption that they are necessarily or never reciprocal.

This conceptual framework stresses the continuum between the taking and regulation of private property. To see how it works, and where the current law falls short, it is best to examine the current law, largely fashioned through Supreme Court decisions, of physical and regulatory takings. Virtually all the errors in the current law underprotect property owners. That systematic bias is not random. Rather, it flows from the mistaken belief that public officials typically act in the public interest whereas private landowners typically do not. This peculiar bias induces courts to let down their guard in dealing with government action. In the area of physical takings, this mistaken attitude manifests itself in the systematic underprotection of property on matters of both just compensation and public use. In regulatory cases, it manifests itself in the extraordinary deference to administrative action that whittles down the protections offered to private property against regulation without compensation. Both errors have enormous consequences for behavior in the political process and the efficient allocation of all types of valuable resources.

Part II   Physical Takings

CHAPTER THREE

A Typology of Physical Takings

As I NOTED IN CHAPTER 2, the most vivid instance of a physical taking occurs when a landowner starts with the permanent and exclusive possession of a plot of land, only to end up with nothing at all. The simplest illustrations arise when the state takes land outright for a fort, road, or post office. Greater difficulties crop up in intermediate cases, when the ownership of a plot of land is divided among several persons. Thus one person may lease a piece of land on which a second person has a mortgage, so that both interests are wiped out when the government takes the underlying parcel. Alternatively, a physical taking is partial if the landowner who starts with complete ownership retains some fractional interest in the parcel after the government has acted, as when the government occupies the land only for a limited period of time, after which it reverts to its original owner.

A physical taking happens when the government action *reduces* the exclusive right of possession that an owner has in a single parcel of land. That loss of exclusive possession does not require the owner to start with outright ownership before the government acts or to end up with nothing at all once the government action is completed. So long as the owner's fractional interest in possession has been reduced, then the government has taken (an interest in) his land. The rules on physical taking apply when a sole owner is forced to share his property, or when one of several joint owners has his interest reduced or eliminated. The differences in degree go only to the measure of compensation, not to the right to be compensated.

Working out the mechanics for dealing with physical takings is more difficult than is commonly supposed. The well-entrenched, complex system of property rights under Anglo-American law means that individuals do not just own land—they own "estates in land," and these estates can be both present and future. Thus one person may hold land for his life, and when he dies a second person may be entitled to hold the same land for her life or forever. Similarly, a landlord holds a reversion that allows him to enter into possession once the tenant's lease has expired. A secured lender (commonly called a mortgagee or lienor) is entitled to take possession of land only after the debtor goes into default.

As a brute economic necessity, the government extinguishes *all* these interests in real property when it takes outright possession of real estate. It follows that each of these instances should always be governed by the somewhat misnamed rules of physical taking even though the remainderman (who is entitled to possession once the current occupant leaves or dies), the landlord, or the mortgagee is necessarily out of possession when the government occupies the land. Yet in practice, these nonpossessory interests receive a somewhat lower level of constitutional protection than that given to an owner, tenant for life, or lessee in possession of land.

Once some physical taking is established, the inquiry switches to other questions. First, does the state have some justification for taking the land without paying any compensation at all? In some cases, the state may wish to seize land its owner uses as an arsenal for dangerous weapons, or to require the destruction of a building whose loose bricks pose a peril to people on the public streets below. The more specific provisions of the criminal code in general govern the former type of case, and I will therefore consider it only tangentially below.

The major controversies with physical takings swirl around two issues. The first is whether the taking is for a public use; if it is not, then it cannot go forward at all, no matter how much money is paid in compensation. Yet once it is concluded that the taking is for public use, the next question is to determine whether the state has paid just compensation. Accordingly, this chapter examines three interrelated topics. First, what is the proper analysis of physical takings? Second, when are these takings for a public use? And last, what does the requirement of just compensation entail?

THE PHYSICAL INVASIONS

Occupation, Damage, and the Parity Principle

Our inquiry into the law of physical takings is shaped by a central interpretive proposition that is conveniently called the parity principle. There is no gap between public and private law. Therefore, whatever actions count as takings when done by a private party also count as takings when done by the state. Finding that a taking has occurred does not necessarily mean that the state must compensate with cash. Rather, it means that no court can avoid the question of whether compensation is owed. To some extent, the case law has adhered to this principle by equating the destruction of property with the taking of property. (Indeed, many state constitutions make the point more emphatically by using the phrase "take or damage" property.) Thus a physical taking, which is "per se" (or automatically) compensable, occurs even if the government occupies only a tiny fraction of private land, such as when the New York Public Utilities Commission ordered an apartment owner, Jean Loretto, to allow a Manhattan cable company to attach a cable and connector box to the roof of her New York apartment house, while leaving the rest of her land undisturbed.

Nor is the finding of a physical taking defeated when a government decree only requires a property owner to allow other people free access to his or her property, without booting the owner off. Thus, in one notable case, the United States told Kaiser Aetna, the owner of a private marina in Hawaii, that boats moored at its facility could gain access to public waters only if it let boats freely enter its marina from public waters. Just asking Kaiser Aetna to share its facilities with the general public triggered the compensation obligation, albeit at a reduced rate, in light of its retained usage. A parallel situation arises whenever the government denies a landowner access to a public highway unless he allows campers to traipse across his back yard. Access to the transportation grid, for obvious reasons of overall efficiency, is included in the bundle of rights in land. It therefore counts as coercion for the state to tell you that you can enjoy access to public roads only if you surrender exclusive possession of your own property. The state cannot force an owner to choose between two entitlements (public access and exclusive possession) any more than a robber may force his victim to choose between her watch and wallet, when she is entitled to both.

A physical taking can also occur when the government occupies land without formally declaring its intentions. Thus when the government builds a mill that permanently floods private land, or authorizes private parties to construct such a mill, it has taken the lands that are flooded, even though it leaves title to the land with its original owner. Sometimes, however, the level of intrusion is too brief to count as a permanent occupation, as when government flood waters quickly recede after disrupting operations on private lands. Of course, this limited flooding counts as a tort when done by any private party; yet current law mistakenly leaves the individual landowner with no constitutional claim for just compensation in the absence of a permanent occupation. But even if that error were rectified, a single intrusion should not, and does not, require the government to pay for perpetual use of the property. Thus the navy does not permanently take private property by firing guns on one or two isolated occasions over someone's private land.

On this score, the expansive reach of the takings clause is at war with the well-established principle of sovereign immunity, which normally holds that the sovereign cannot be sued in state or federal court for a breach of contract or the commission of a tort. Ironically, sovereign immunity is not mentioned in the Constitution, although the *Federalist* papers treat it as one of the background English norms that was carried forward by implication into our Constitution. Yet some compromise is imperative, for if sovereign immunity covers all government actions, then the takings clause would be a dead letter: no one would have the right to sue to vindicate his nominal right to compensation. Hence the Supreme Court draws a fine line between events, like flooding, that result in a permanent occupation for which compensation is owed, and isolated incidents, such as accidental sonic booms, to which sovereign immunity applies. Yet, history aside, there is no principled reason why the government's sovereign status should insulate it from liability for one-time damages to strangers. Ironically, this comprehensive view of the takings clause won out when Congress adopted the Federal Torts Claims

Act in 1946, which, with exceptions for various "discretionary functions" of the regulatory state, holds the government liable for its torts in the same fashion as any private citizen, just as the parity principle requires.

Overflights, Oil and Gas, and Wildlife: Coping with the Prisoner's Dilemma

In the early years of commercial aviation, landowners frequently asked courts either to enjoin planes from flying over land or to award cash compensation for the entry into their airspace. Those intrusions could be either in the upper airspace only, near ground level (airspace the owner could actually use), or just close enough for the noise and vibration to cause cracks, settling, and other property damage. The established common-law rule is a Latin mouthful: "Cuius est solum euis est usque ad coelum et usque ad inferos" (whoever owns the land also owns to the heavens and the depths).

Under the *ad coelum* portion of the rule, all three forms of overflight are prima facie wrongful. But the consequences of keeping the planes out differ radically in these three contexts. Let landowners stop the flights in the upper airspace, and it marks the end of commercial aviation, because multiple holdout problems among squabbling ground owners would prevent any aircraft from flying across Manhattan, let alone the country. The simplest way to avoid this unpalatable result is to reject the ancient common-law *ad coelum* rule as a mistake, and "redefine" the landowner's property right to cover only that airspace over which he could exercise effective possession.

That ad hoc revision of property rights niftily "solve" this particular problem, but at the cost of inviting the state to invoke this sleight of hand everywhere else, until all property rights are defined out of existence. Why couldn't the state also decree that the landowner no longer owns the land under a glide path, or within 100 feet of a public road? The better approach is to treat historical air rights as fully protected, and thereafter to determine what compensation, if any, a landowner should receive for these state-sanctioned invasions. Unlike the definitional approach, this two-step inquiry yields different results for upper and lower airspace.

In upper airspace, individuals lose no *use* value when stripped of their right to exclude. Ironically, any right to blockade quickly becomes worthless when thousands of other landowners demand compensation for any entry into their respective airspaces. More formally, the overflight cases give rise to the classic prisoner's dilemma game: every surface owner, if left to his own devices, would charge hefty tolls, even though all would be better off individually if the only regulation of the upper airspace came when the Federal Aviation Authority creates highways in the sky. Using state coercion for the upper airspace overcomes the massive coordination problem among acquisitive surface owners. By opening up upper airspace to flight, all ground owners gain, both directly and indirectly, from the personal and commercial advantages of air flight. The gains from open use supply the implicit in-kind compensation to make the transaction win–win all the way around. The courts should not award any side payments, because even huge administrative outlays could never identify which landowners should be net payers and which net recipients. The enormous gains all around make it imperative to ignore the fine points of uneven distribution.

The analysis of invasions of the lower airspace takes a different path. Now, it should not matter whether the flights are overhead or nearby. Either way, the endless vibrations and noise cause a huge and distinctive diminution in land values. No ploy about the definition of "property" should allow the state to escape the obligation to compensate for these overflights. Current law recognizes this disproportionate impact for direct, trespassory overflights, but invokes the tenuous tort/taking line to mistakenly refuse to compensate landowners outside the flight path who nonetheless suffer property damage from the din. These second-class citizens can get compensation only through legislative grace, which is at best partial and erratic.

The overflight cases highlight an instructive pattern that will dominate the regulatory takings cases in the next section: if the benefits of a given innovation are widespread, and its burdens concentrated on an unfortunate few, then by all means, let the state pay cash compensation to even out the score. If both benefits and burdens are equally dispersed, then implicit in-kind compensation meets the constitutional standard of just compensation for all comers, especially when the overall gains are huge. But clever lawyers cannot "solve" the problem by allowing the legislature to just "redefine" property rights in ways that undermine preexisting entitlements. That seductive tactic inverts the relationship between the Constitution and the legislature by making the latter paramount over the former.

Ad Inferos

A similar analysis applies to the *ad inferos* part of the rule, which deals with ownership below the surface. At first blush, the efficient mining of minerals or extraction of oil and gas from underground pools looks to have little in common with organizing air rights. In fact, the exact same conceptual framework governs both. To set the stage, first note that normally the surface owner has the exclusive right to remove natural resources below his own land. This rule of acquisition for hard minerals presents relatively few problems, as these are necessarily fixed in location, making it fairly easy to separate them from minerals on neighboring land. (There is an important exception for certain minerals, like silver, found only in meandering seams: in these cases, the customary rule, to reward investigation, assigns ownership of the entire seam to the person who first discovers any part of it.)

As applied to oil and gas, the *ad inferos* rule generates a prohibition against "slant" drilling, which solves the first problem of ownership. It secures clear title to the driller who removes the oil from beneath the earth, which allows for refining and sale. Yet this variation of the first possession rule is subject to institutional weaknesses not found with hard minerals. Oil and gas are "fugacious," in that they circulate under the lands of many surface owners. The uncoordinated drilling of oil and gas wells therefore leads to massive overextraction, as self-interested surface owners form a "picket fence" by drilling many wells straight down at the boundary line of their property, both to protect their own stake and to siphon off oil and gas from their neighbors. This behavior increases costs, raises the risk of land collapse, and reduces output—a ruinous trifecta.

One response to this major inefficiency is to redefine property rights so that only certain people remain entitled to drill. But who should be entitled and why? As with the overflights, this open-ended strategy of redefinition is overkill when more focused techniques better counteract this version of the prisoner's dilemma. On the cost side, first let the state reduce the number of wells that extract oil and gas. Fewer wells mean lower costs and less disruption of the field. The ideal strategy opens only those wells that would be drilled if a single profit-maximizing person owned the entire field. Think here of a nine-square tic-tac-toe board in which the efficient solution has a single well in the middle of a center square. But using one well does not compensate others for their loss of the right to drill. That goal can be achieved by paying some fraction of the net royalties to each surface owner as compensation for the loss of his right to drill. Calculating the proper allocation for each surface owner often raises measurement difficulties, because oil and gas fields are often deep in the center and shallow at the edges. One simple approach calculates the respective shares by determining the fraction of the total barrels of oil that is under the land of each individual owner. A more sophisticated but less reliable technique resorts to game theory. This approach first estimates the "threat position" of each landowner: the fraction of the total field that each owner could gain by drilling selfishly at his boundary lines. Each person then gets the same fraction of the larger output, net of common expenses. At this point, we replicate the outcome in the upper airspace: each surface owner gains proportionately with others, within the limits of measurement error.

There are two important corollaries to this basic position on common pool assets. The first is that the process of improvement through regulation can be done multiple times. Thus, suppose the state first imposes one scheme of regulation, which has the desired effect of improving the lot of everyone with an interest in the common pool from (to keep things simple) 5 to 10. At this point, 10 becomes the new baseline against which further social changes are made. That decision means that it is impermissible for the state to introduce some new scheme that moves everyone from 10 to 7, even though they still remain above the initial 5. But the initial shift does not preclude any further system of regulation that moves all individuals from 10 to 15, which in turn becomes the new baseline against which further regulation is measured. There is no necessary upper bound to social improvements that common pool regulation can achieve.

The second corollary to the basic position on common pool assets is illustrated in the famous 1899 case, *Ohio Oil Co. v. Indiana,* involving the regulation of both oil and gas extraction. The Supreme Court did not examine the full economic consequences of the scheme, and thus allowed it to go forward, even though its rules favored—as our political instincts should suspect—the in-state gas producers, who profited at the expense of out-of-state oil producers, whom the regulation left worse off. To be sure, this takings analysis justifies regulations that produce proportionate gains for all players. That endorsement is surely muted when the gains in question are larger for one side than the other. But this takings analysis unambiguously condemns regulations, such as those at issue here, that result in a transfer of wealth between groups that leaves one side worse off than before. Disguised transfers of wealth between groups in common pool regimes should be caught by the takings clause.

Fish and Game

The same common pool problem evident with oil and gas fields also arises with fish and game, because uncontrolled fishing and hunting, whether on private or public property, frequently leads to the destruction of the underlying stock. Defenders of property rights are said to be blind to that risk, insofar as they treat the right to acquire wildlife by capture as a property right, good against the world, protected under the takings clause. Often the critics deny any such right in order to give the state a free hand to protect all forms of wildlife. As with air rights, they claim that the state may simply redefine property rights so that it now owns all things that were once owned by no one. Using that power lets the government wipe out fishermen and hunters without paying a dime in compensation.

There is little doubt that the introduction of sensible catch or bag limits helps preserve various forms of wildlife over the long haul. Yet those regulations do not offer a counterexample to the general approach taken here, even if the right to capture is protected under the takings clause. Rather, we can plot a middle path through the extremes, for there is no need to ignore property rights in order to preserve wildlife against this well-known tragedy of the commons. The full account of the common pool recognizes that the state can take anyone's right to acquire wildlife so long as it supplies just compensation in cash or in kind, including access rights under a permit system that promises long-term stability for the underlying resource. Consistent with this approach, the state may limit by statute or regulation the total capture of fish and game, so long as it allocates some *fraction* of the sustainable yield to those presently in the business. The current users of the commons, however, should not be entitled to the entire increase from state regulation, as they are with oil and gas, where no outsider has free entry to the underground fields. After all, in the case of the unregulated commons, the shares of incumbent hunters and fishermen are always subject to erosion by new entrants. Accordingly, the entry rights of new parties should also be recognized under any statutory realignment of these wildlife regimes.

In effect, regulation should follow a two-part scheme. First, some portion of the catch limits should be allocated to the current resource users, in order to leave them as well off as they were under the common-law regime of open capture. Second, the remaining portion of the increased stock should be available for the state to distribute by auction or license to late entrants. This compromise solution gives the incumbents a statutory claim that functions as in-kind compensation for their loss of the common-law rights of acquisition. Yet by allowing the state to distribute the surplus, the takings law does nothing to prevent the state from adopting the most appropriate institutional arrangements for the management and use of common pool resources.

As already noted, physical takings become a bit trickier when real property has been divided into multiple interests. The issue is of vital importance, because much of the economic value of land derives from the ability to divide it among multiple persons. Even though most people think that they own their land outright, they often have it encumbered with leases, mortgages, easements, or covenants. Any legal rule that makes partial interests in real property more vulnerable to government expropriation in effect clogs an owner's right to alienate property, thereby reducing its overall value. The takings law therefore has to address these various arrangements, which it does with mixed success. Here are three examples.

Mortgages

Frequently, creditors receive liens on both real and personal property as security for their loans. That property interest allows them to sell the underlying property to satisfy an outstanding claim, returning the remaining funds, less expenses, to the owner. In one famous takings case, *Armstrong v. United States*, a supplier of materials used in the construction of navy personnel boats had a valid lien under Maine law against their hulls. Rather than pay off the lien to gain clear title to the boats, the navy simply sailed the ships out of Maine territorial waters to dissolve the lien. The language of physical takings doesn't exactly capture this situation, for the United States didn't take the boat, which it owned, but it did take a nonpossessory interest in the boat—the lien—which it did not own. Justice Harlan, in dissent, thought that sovereign immunity allowed this ruse to succeed, but Justice Black, writing for the majority, vindicated Armstrong's takings claim with this often-quoted sentence: "The Fifth Amendment's guarantee that private property shall not be taken for a public use without just compensation was designed to bar Government from forcing some people alone to bear public burdens which, in all fairness and justice, should be borne by the public as a whole." The public that gets the use of the ships had to pay off the materialman.

The proportionality principle was not new in *Armstrong*. During the depression, for example, that principle had profound implications for the real estate market, when federal monetary policy unwisely produced a major deflation of around 30 percent by cutting the money supply. For landowners who borrowed money on their property, that deflation increased their debt in real terms, because each nominal dollar was worth more than before. Both the states and Congress entered the fray with debtor-relief legislation to prevent lenders from taking possession of the underlying land when the mortgage was not repaid. In the 1934 case of *Home Building & Loan Association v. Blaisdell*, the Supreme Court sustained the Minnesota Mortgage Moratorium on the dubious ground that its one-year delay in foreclosure was justified by the temporary emergency, even though no compensation was supplied. But a year later, in *Louisville Joint Stock Land Bank v. Radford*, the Court struck down Congress's original Frazier-Lemke Farm Bankruptcy Act, which had allowed the federal courts both to reduce the size of the debt and to impose a five-year moratorium on repayment. These cases are harder than *Armstrong*, because the postponed collection is only a partial destruction of the lien, not its total dissolution. Nonetheless, unless the government compensates for that loss, the taking should be blocked. In language that anticipated *Armstrong*, Justice Brandeis, writing for the unanimous Court in *Louisville Joint Stock Land Bank*, did not allow progressive instincts to beat back a takings claim: "For the Fifth Amendment commands that, however great the Nation's need, private property shall not be thus taken even for a wholly public use without just compensation. If the public interest requires, and permits, the taking of property of individual mortgagees in order to relieve the necessities of individual mortgagors, resort must be had to proceedings by eminent domain; so that, through taxation, the burden of the relief afforded in the public interest may be borne by the public."

This categorical distinction between major and minor dislocations is not tenable. By blocking foreclosure, all mortgage moratoria statutes necessarily take some portion of the lender's interest in the underlying property. To offset that taking, the key question is whether the statutes gave the creditor either additional interest or greater security to compensate for the loss of rights. Many mortgage moratoria statutes, like the Frazier-Lemke Act, failed to achieve this goal. Unsurprisingly, the banks, which had to pay off their demand deposits, frequently failed, creating rippling distortions throughout the system. That disastrous outcome cannot, however, be clearly laid at the doorstep of the moratoria statutes. The real damage was done by the deflation, because it entails a large transfer in wealth from debtors to creditors, which in an integrated economy can never be worked out by a readjustment of the rights between them. The only workable solution depends on a stable monetary policy that avoids, above all, unanticipated fluctuation in currency value. But since no court can control the money supply, no judicial decision can counteract the mischief in bad monetary policy, no matter how it decides the moratoria cases.

In contrast, the postponement of debt repayment for additional interest and security works better when money is stable. Modern bankruptcy law, for example, often forces secured creditors to forgo taking possession of their property in exchange for additional security and further interest payments. The underlying theory is that the property in question is critical to the reorganization of an ongoing business. But the risk remains that the interest will not compensate the lender for the additional risks, especially when the underlying property could depreciate when left in the hands of the debtor. But in all these cases, the normative objective is intelligible, even if hard to achieve: to allow debtors to resist loss of property so long as they compensate lenders for their additional risk.

Future Interests

Takings law also protects future interests in land. If an owner divides property between a landlord and tenant, the government can't take the entire property for free just because neither person owns it outright. Rather, it must pay each party to the extent of the interest, for a voluntary division of land neither increases nor diminishes the rights both owners have against the government. The contrary rule would inhibit these useful transactions by exposing both parties to the risk of confiscation. The takings law thus allows economic efficiency, not the risk of government misbehavior, to determine the ownership of land.

This principle was sorely tested when Congress passed the 1983 Rails-to-Trails Act. Grants to railroads often gave them rights of way over land that lasted only "so long as it was used for railway purposes." Under the typical grant, the land reverts to its owner once the track is removed from the rail bed. The 1983 Act decreed that the roadbed remained with the state indefinitely for use as a bicycle path even after the tracks were abandoned, on the minuscule chance that some railroad would lay new tracks in the future. In a Vermont case, the Preseaults, whose land was crossed by an old railway line, were turned into trespassers under this statute, which allowed the state to physically block them from crossing the bikepath from one side of their land to the other. Only after bitter litigation was the United States forced to pay the Preseaults for turning the land over to Vermont on expiration of the railroad's easement. Again the parity principle applies. To be sure, the United States did not force the Preseaults off their land. They only refused to allow them to return under the terms of the original railroad grant. Surely any private person who tried to keep land after his easement expired would have been slapped down without a thought. So if Congress wants to devote those roadbeds for bicyclists, then it can condemn the land by paying just compensation.

Rent Control

Physical takings loom still larger with traditional rent control statutes, where the limited duration of the tenant's occupation is front and center. The standard common-law rule requires a tenant to vacate premises at the expiration of the lease. If the tenant "holds over" thereafter, he is subject to eviction, and in the interim he is required to pay either the rent specified in the lease or the market value, whichever is greater. This tough measure prevents the tenant from profiting by his wrongful actions no matter which way the market moves. Rent control statutes overturn this uniform rule by allowing the tenant to stay put after the lease has expired, while paying rent that the state unilaterally sets *below* current market value. Older rent control statutes chose a fixed amount, without regard to inflation; modern rent stabilization laws peg rent increases to inflation, without allowing further rent increases for surges in market demand. In both cases, the tenant benefits exclusively from market appreciation. None of the landlord's service obligations are eliminated.

Clearly much is amiss. Start with whether rent control statutes count as physical takings. The original rent control cases reached the Supreme Court in the aftermath of World War I, before the distinction between possessory and regulatory takings came into vogue. In one early case, *Block v. Hirsh*, Justice Holmes justified the sharp restrictions on rent as a proper public response to the rapid increase in demand for rental housing in Washington, D.C., brought on by the influx of government workers during World War I. The complete analysis plays out differently. Under the parity principle, it is clear that the state takes the property by keeping the landlord from regaining possession of his property, as in the rails-to-trails case. It hardly matters that the property stays in the hands of the original tenant. It is just as though the state occupied the land itself and then transferred all its rights and duties to the sitting tenant for free, without the consent of the landlord, who is forced to accept the low rent. That maneuver only compounds the problem, because a transfer of discrete premises to a single occupant hardly satisfies the public use requirement. Because the new rental is fixed at below market value, the proper compensation for the loss should equal, at the very least, the present (i.e. discounted) value of the future savings that the tenant receives under rent control. If the state wants to pick up that tab from general revenues, then the landlord has no complaint. Unfortunately, no rent control system ever forces the government to pay a plug nickel. Rent control demotes the landlord from an owner, who gains when the premises appreciate, to a creditor, who gets at best a fixed return—and takes all the downside—without relieving him of any of the landlord's duties.

Further evidence of how rent control transfers wealth from landlords to tenants becomes clear with a scheme that many communities use for the leased pads for mobile homes. Local ordinances commonly prevent the pad owner from evicting a mobile home–owner on the termination of the lease. But that owner is free to sell his mobile home to a buyer of his choice, who then inherits the right to use the site. If all that were sold were the home, sales prices would decline over time to reflect depreciation and aging. Usually, however, the sales price *rises* because it covers both the old mobile home *and* the economic benefit from the perpetual lease of the pad at below-market rentals.

The local ordinance allows the holdover tenant to keep his mobile home on someone else's site. Unfortunately, in *Yee v. City of Escondido*, a case that involved the leasing of mobile home pads, Justice O'Connor put the blame squarely on the landowner's shoulders: "put bluntly," the "tenants were invited by the [landowners], not forced upon them by the government." This argument is plain wrong. The landowner's invitation was of course for only a limited time, and the government forced the landlord to allow the tenant to remain. Staying after being told to leave has been a trespass since time immemorial. Why? Because in every voluntary transaction, the time dimension is key to the definition of the property right. It is absurd to say that if you invite guests to use your summer home for the weekend, the law could make you let them stay rent-free for life.

Socially, rent control scars every community where it holds sway. If landlords cannot raise rents, they will lower quality. Over time, neighborhoods stagnate for the want of fresh capital. Simultaneously, rent control has dramatic effects on the distribution of wealth. As Nora Ephron, who is no Chicago economist, relates in a *New Yorker* story on her own experience, the system spawns a peculiar culture in which the haves luxuriate in apartments for a fraction of their market value, while everyone else scrambles to pick up the crumbs at artificially inflated prices. A system put forward to protect the little guy perversely entrenches the well-connected. New York's rent control culture encourages universities and other employers to build their own residences so that their faculty and staff do not have to face the perils of an over-heated market in which desperate apartment seekers "schmear" (the local term) the super's palm to get early access to a vacant apartment, or pay key money in multiples of the monthly rent to the outgoing tenant. Rent control invites sitting tenants to choose strategic roommates or make advantageous subleases. It encourages landlords to use Gestapo tactics to pry tenants from their homes.

Once entrenched, these systems are hard to repeal at the local level, because of the voting power of local tenants. To be sure, these tenants can support statutes that exempt new construction from rent control. But their effect is ambiguous. Zoning laws make new construction difficult, even for developers who will be attracted by the high rents in the unregulated sector. These developers are wary of building rental units out of fear that in time their tenants will agitate for the protection of some rent control laws. But throughout it all, the same local voters who are willing to cap the rents paid to others have never accepted price controls on the sale of apartments or homes that they own.

These layers of deceit and intrigue are not immutable facts of nature. Apartments turn over without incident in Chicago and many other cities without rent control. In most cases, moreover, political forces are sufficient to prevent the adoption of new rent control statutes, given that New York has long been the poster child of all that can go wrong. But on this issue at least, there is no principled reason to wait for a long overdue political solution. The major dislocations in local rental markets arise because rent control statutes run roughshod over fundamental property rights. If the state had to pick up the differential by giving direct subsidies to all protected tenants, rich or poor, the present system, where subsidies are unrelated to income or poverty, would immediately collapse for want of public support, which is as it should be. Justice Brandeis's words on disproportionate impact in the mortgage moratoria cases ring true: constitutionally, the state must always use public funding to secure public benefits. Remember that the just compensation requirement has two functions. It first compensates individuals whose property is taken for worthy social projects. In addition, it imposes a vital price constraint on government so that unworthy social projects, such as rent control, never get off the ground.

. . .

CHAPTER FOUR

Public Use

A TOOTHLESS DOCTRINE

Under modern law, at least at the federal level, the public use requirement has few teeth. Today's conventional wisdom holds that so long as the state acts for a legitimate public purpose—such as slum clearance—it does not matter that the property taken from A ends up in the hands of B, when both are private parties. The stated incidental social benefits, which include everything from blight removal to newer buildings, to a bigger tax base, justify removing sitting tenants whose sole protection comes from receiving compensation—which, as will become evident, falls far short of any proper measure.

This broad deference stems in large part from the confident judgment that public officials need sufficient running room to pursue the ideals of sound planning. Deciding how to rebuild a downtown area is thought to lie outside the scope of legal expertise, so that courts should confine themselves to ratifying the outcomes of a political process that can take advantage of extensive public hearings and expert planning reports. The opposition to this view, which has intensified after the 2005 *Kelo* decision, stems from two main concerns. First, it does not square with the text of the takings clause to read "for public use" to mean "for any conceivable indirect public benefit." After all, any ingenious government agency can always manufacture some conceivable indirect benefit from any transfer of property from A to B: the more massive the program, the easier the job.

The second objection to the current practice is more instrumental. The idealized view of planning bodies working tirelessly for the public good badly misses how parochial local interest groups use planning to gain unfair competitive advantage over commercial rivals. One recent scheme (on which I have consulted) that Congress ratified in the Wright Amendment Reform Act of 2006 authorized Dallas and Fort Worth to condemn and then demolish private terminal facilities at Love Field Airport in order to solidify the joint monopoly position of American and Southwest Airlines. Yet there is no explanation of how the public benefits from higher prices for air transportation. So the defenders of the Act point to supposed environmental benefits from the restriction of air traffic, without explaining why their flights should be left untouched while those of their competitors are grounded. We can only hope that this scheme will be struck down under the one safeguard that survives the *Kelo* decision. Programs that result from private agreements, as this one did, do not receive the same deference as comprehensive plans, however unwise, that follow extensive community oversight and review.

The aggressive behavior of local governments is further revealed in another recent case, *Didden v. Village of Port Chester.* The town of Port Chester named Greg Wasser as the developer in charge of its redevelopment effort. When Bart Didden and Dominick Bologna proposed to put a CVS pharmacy on land they owned in the development zone, Wasser said he would go along only if they paid him $800,000 or gave him a half interest in the project. When Didden and Bologna rebuffed him, Wasser got Port Chester to condemn the land the next day, without hearings, so that he could reap the profits from putting a Walgreen's on the same site. A federal court held that this form of government action satisfied the public use requirement. Yet, strangely enough, its brief opinion was devoid of reasons beyond the claim that it was inappropriate to "second-guess" the town's action, which it concluded was "neither a constitutional exaction in the form of extortion nor an equal protection violation." No explanation followed. This sorry form of private abuse that took place under the shelter of the *Kelo* decision is reminiscent of the tax collectors under Louis XIV. The Supreme Court declined to review the case.

WHERE THE LAW WENT WRONG

The basic lesson should not be forgotten because of a naïve faith in good government. Sadly, the politicians who are given an inch take a mile. Putting real teeth into the public use requirement would halt this trend by giving landowners confidence that they will be able to reap the benefits of their past investments and current plans. A tougher public use limitation also reduces the scope for political horse trades that benefit insiders at the expense of the less-well-connected citizens. Just where did the law go wrong?

Use by the Public

Let's start with the easy cases. The paradigmatic case of taking land for a public use is, well, taking it for the use of the public. This formulation connotes the free and open access of a public highway, but is surely not so limited. Public toll roads count as public uses, even if some people cannot afford the tolls. It would be odd to construe the public use requirement so narrowly as to prevent rational pricing through user fees, forcing the state to rely on less efficient modes of funding, such as gasoline taxes (which poorly correlate with use) or general revenues (which don't correlate at all). It is quite sufficient that all are invited to pay according to a uniform set of tariffs, including those that accurately reflect the disproportionate damage from heavy vehicles. At the opposite extreme, military installations are public uses, even though the public is kept off to preserve national security.

Both types of public use cases leave little role for the courts. It is easy to decide what counts as a highway or military base, so burdens of proof just don't matter. Of course, the wisdom of committing public funds to these projects requires a cost-benefit analysis that lies with the political branches, whether it results in the construction of a tasteful downtown area like Chicago's Millennium Park, or a horrific displacement of ordinary people as seen in Robert Moses's manic road-building, neighborhood-busting projects of yore in New York City. No principled account of the takings clause gives courts the power to initiate, finance, or oversee any public project. The constraints on budget-breaking projects are primarily political, subject only to limitation by the state's obligation to pay just compensation.

The analysis becomes more complex wherever condemnation power is used in the first instance to benefit private owners. Suppose the state condemns property for the construction of a railroad that is both privately owned and operated. In this context, a narrow definition of public *use* does not have much appeal. The land needed for the railroad lies in separate hands, and it must be "assembled," or placed under common ownership, to be of value for its intended use. Railroads are long and skinny, and typically the rights of way for them are in the hands of multiple people, often farmers of the land. Any assembly of rights of way for this project often requires state condemnation power to overcome the endless holdouts—a variation of the air rights case. Yet it would be plain foolish to insist that Amtrak run all railways because only the government can condemn land. Nor is that result required, because public *use* does not necessarily entail either public ownership or management. It is sufficient that the private railroad is subject to common carrier obligations to admit all comers on reasonable and nondiscriminatory terms, as has commonly been done.

Assembly and Necessity

The "public use" language is put to a sterner test when state power is essential to assemble the property for key facilities *not* subject to a common carrier duty to take all comers. The issue came to a head in the second half of the nineteenth century under the Mill Acts, which allowed local governments to flood private farmland in order to raise dams needed to power private mills. Physically, the number of such dams along any river was strictly limited. Unilateral construction by multiple private owners leads to resource dissipation, so public administrative procedures were created to decide who could build a dam and how high it could be. Some gristmills, in fact, had common carrier status, but many did not. Nonetheless, the courts held that this private use satisfied the public use requirement, because of the great benefits these mills offered to their communities. There were, of course, real distributional concerns. Why should the party that forces the transaction get all the gain? To obviate that outcome, some statutes set compensation at 150 percent of market value to give condemned landowners a piece of the overall gain, at the cost of blocking some projects that are only worthwhile if compensation is set below the statutory amount.

Other cases echoed that cautious extension of public use to public benefit. Thus in the early part of the twentieth century, the Supreme Court held in *Strickley v. Highland Boy Gold Mining Co.* that a state took land for a public use when it allowed a mine owner to construct a tramway over the scrub land of a neighbor without his consent, in order to get his ore to a railroad track that could be reached in no other way. The Supreme Court was uncomfortable with allowing the state to create this private easement, given the public use limitation. But it grudgingly held that the necessity of the physical locale allowed the state to suspend the operation of the usual right to exclude, much as the common law does in cases of private necessity, where a boat in distress is able to moor at the pier of a stranger so long as its owner pays just compensation for the damage caused.

Urban Renewal, Beautification, and Land Reform

In this new context, however, we *do* have to worry about the proper judicial standard of review, because the term "public benefit" suggests that the state has no right to force wasteful exchanges. How closely should courts look at the relationship between cost and benefit? The problem was not acute in these cases because the mills and overhead trams both pass muster under a pretty high standard of review, especially when compensation over market value is required. So the skeptic now asks whether, once Pandora's box has been opened, courts can find any limits to public use after the literal meaning of the term has been rejected. More modern cases have found all sorts of ingenious reasons for permitting aggressive government efforts in large-scale urban planning and renewal. In the 1930s, the New York high court held that tearing down serviceable private homes and businesses to put up public housing projects counted as a legitimate public use. But note the shift in emphasis. No longer did the finding of public use turn on whether state power was needed to overcome a market failure in the form of a major holdout problem. Unlike mills and trams, building plots for more modest projects are readily available at multiple locations. Instead, the newer view rests on the far more disputable proposition that unregulated private housing markets shortchange poor tenants. This proposition was congenial to the progressive intellectuals who powered the New Deal.

New York's expansive view of public use received its federal imprimatur in 1954, when a unanimous Supreme Court held in *Berman v. Parker* that Berman's well-maintained department store, located on the impoverished east side of Washington, D.C., could be torn down as part of a comprehensive slum clearance plan. Justice Douglas echoed his progressive forebears by insisting: "It is within the power of the legislature to determine that the community should be beautiful as well as healthy, spacious as well as clean, well-balanced as well as carefully patrolled." The possibility that Washington could remove "blight" in smaller doses was treated as a choice better made by the legislature and its expert planning commissions.

In some sense, Berman's vulnerability to condemnation depended on an implicit understanding that his department store was located in a blighted neighborhood. But nothing in the logic of Douglas's opinion tethered public use to blight, as opposed to the more inclusive objectives of urban renewal and economic development. In the 1981 case of *Poletown Neighborhood Council v. City of Detroit*, the Michigan supreme court allowed, over a fierce dissent, the state to condemn the entire community of Poletown— houses, businesses, clubs, churches, and more—in order to keep a General Motors plant (which of course never lived up to its inflated advance billing) within city limits. This outcome is light-years away from the earlier mill and tram cases.

The basic argument for some relaxation of the public use requirement is that land assembly cannot take place in a coherent fashion if each of the individual landowners can hold out for a high price. This assembly problem accounts for the willingness of the courts to go one step beyond the *Berman* blight control rationale, for it is not possible for public parties, which must deliberate openly over these plans, to adopt the same secret and imaginative tactics available to private developers, who routinely employ shills and straw corporations to acquire contiguous properties. For a wonderful illustration of how far resourceful brokers can go within the law, it is well worth reading Peter Hellman's inspired 1974 *New York* account of how the then First National City Bank assembled thirty-one parcels under separate ownership in the heart of the Manhattan midtown for its splashy new headquarters. Yet by the same token, why is it necessary to build a huge General Motors plant in Poletown when lots of nearby farmland is available for the asking, without these dislocations? Most modern assembly cases stretch the notion of location-specific necessity far beyond its original contours.

Nor did the beat stop there. Some three years after *Poletown*, the United States Supreme Court unanimously sustained Hawaii's 1967 Land Reform Act, whereby a tenant of leased property was allowed to buy out the landlord's interest by depositing an earmarked sum with the Hawaiian Housing Authority (HHA) to fund the condemnation of the landlord's interest—followed by its prompt transfer to the current tenant. Frank Midkiff sued when the HHA tried to acquire his land under this Act. The scheme did not force Midkiff off his land—only his right to reenter at the end of the lease was lost. But that detail did not excuse the Reform

Act's prearranged transfer from A to B. Undeterred by the obvious, Justice O'Connor held that Hawaii's statute passed muster because it was "rationally related to any conceivable public purpose." This purpose was found in the need to control what she perceived as an economic oligopoly owing to the large fraction of developed land owned by the Bishop's Estate, the successor in title to the extensive holdings of the Kamehameha Hawaiian royal family, and other large landowners. Yet the economic deviation between a pure competitive market and the Oahu market, where twenty-two landowners held 72.5 percent of the titles, is so negligible under standard antitrust tests as to defy measure. Nor did O'Connor point a finger at Hawaii's restrictive zoning law, which further squeezed Hawaii's overheated real estate market.

It was against this backdrop that the controversial five-to-four 2005 *Kelo* decision allowed New London to force Susette Kelo and fourteen other landowners from their homes as part of its comprehensive development plan. In one sense, *Kelo*'s outcome was not strictly compelled, because the "public use" language could have been read to allow condemnation only in cases of supposed blight or supposed oligopoly. By any ordinary definition, the modest homes in *Kelo* were not blighted. Nor could anyone describe these embattled landowners as oligopolists. But Justice Stevens ran with the broad language in *Berman* and *Midkiff*, even though New London had articulated *no* definite plans for use of the site of the condemned houses. Now that little people were hurt, the public furor combined the populist suspicion of developers on the Left with the respect for property rights on the Right.

The deeper question, however, is whether there is any way to jump off the trolley one hundred years after the Court had approved private mills and trams. Fortunately, there is. Any decision to condemn private lands for private use turns on two factors: the

Susette Kelo outside her New London home. Photo by Spencer Platt/
Getty Images.

nature of the condemned land and the public necessity for this
condemnation. Farmlands and scrublands hold little or no subjective value for their owners, making their market value an accurate reflection of the owner's loss. By the same token, the
holdout potential is enormous, because neither the mill owner nor
the mine owner has any flexibility to relocate his place of business. That combination of low subjective value and great holdout
potential minimizes the risk of corruption, which is why those
condemnations received the guarded blessing of an earlier Supreme Court.

Berman, Poletown, and *Kelo* present the opposite profile. The
owners' subjective value in their homes, businesses, and communities are high. Tying compensation to loss of market value
systematically results in valuation that is too low. Yet urban re-

newal programs do not have anything like the geographical specificity found in the mill and mine cases. In *Kelo*, for example, every major building project could have gone forward as planned on closed naval and water purification facilities (totaling about 90 acres) that New London already owned, without taking any of the private homes. So the two values are inverted: subjective value is high, and holdout potential is low. The text of the takings clause does not differentiate the public use requirement by the type of property taken. But the rapid expansion in the use of eminent domain powers—beyond the narrow cases of taking for use by the public—cries out for that inquiry, lest urban renewal continue to run amok.

So the best approach here is to accept the constitutional trade-off that allows the taking only when the loss in subjective value is small and the locational necessities are great. But by the same token we should deny the state the right to take when the balance runs the opposite way. It is always difficult to build a constitutional edifice from three small words, "for public use," without leaving any play in the joints. But even if those words are not confined to their literal meaning, extending their reach should mean an uphill battle, and not *Kelo*'s downhill glide.

But what about the modern penchant for planning? In general we should repress it at least when it is done in the name of economic development. Restricted public rights to condemn encourage more investment in private property, the surest way to prevent blight. And remember, private developers who can assemble large parcels of lands are often shut out by restrictive zoning ordinances like those in Hawaii. Relax the one form of state coercion (zoning), and the need for the second (condemnation) is diminished. Yet even so, some large inner-city projects might flounder. But so what? Why do factories, huge malls, or home offices have to be in cities at all? Use larger tracts in nearby locations, without driving ordinary people from their homes and businesses. Urban shoppers can purchase consumer goods at smaller shops, strip malls, and today, online, even if the mega-stores are out of reach. The public outrage after *Kelo* arose in response to the arrogance of planners. Virtually every state in the union has on its legislative plate some limitation on *Kelo*. Several state courts have read the public use language in their own constitutions far more narrowly than the Supreme Court reads that phrase in the U.S. Constitution. Prior to *Kelo*, Michigan unanimously denied the legislature the power to condemn property solely for economic development, but left untouched the slum clearance and blight removal cases. More recently, in the post-*Kelo* era, the Ohio supreme court, in a strongly worded unanimous opinion, held that Ohio's constitution required "heightened scrutiny" for condemnation on grounds of blight. And for good reason. Aggressive planners have found blight in irregular streets, old homes, diverse neighbors, and, in one instance, in leaves on a tennis court—so much so that the Ohio supreme court complained that upper-crust communities from Beacon Hill in Boston to Tribeca in New York to Nob Hill in San Francisco were ripe for condemnation. It should have added that in any event, condemnation is not the proper remedy for blight. If a home becomes really dilapidated so that falling mortar is a peril to neighbors, then the city should not buy the property, but give the owner an opportunity to cure the defect before ripping down the structure as a public nuisance, and without compensation, under the traditional definition of the police power. But the city should not take title to blighted property when this lesser remedy is available. Cutting "public use" down to size won't solve all the problems of urban development, for there are many projects, however unwise, that meet even the narrowest definition of public use. In these cases, the battlefront shifts from public use to the question of just compensation. As is always the case, the amount of compensation that the state must award will determine its willingness to go ahead with various projects that fall within its constitutional purview. That topic is the subject of Part II of this book.

CHAPTER FIVE

Unjust Compensation

MARKET VALUE AND BEYOND

The just compensation required under the takings clause can come in two forms. The first is the implicit in-kind compensation that played such a large role in the earlier discussion of takings, and now reenters the analysis with regulatory takings. Second, there is the explicit cash compensation that is typically owed whenever the government takes outright possession of all or part of private land. In these cases, which are the subject of this chapter, this second compensation question should be, but often isn't, straightforward. Setting cash compensation correctly, moreover, is critical to the sound functioning of our condemnation system. The just compensation rules set the prices for government initiatives. As in ordinary markets, these prices alter the demand (by government) for taking land. Set those prices too low, and the government will snap up land that is better left in the hands of owners. Set them too high, and government will abandon worthwhile public projects unless eager landowners, hat in hand, can engineer the taking of their land. The errors matter in both directions, but they are not of equal magnitude, because hard-strapped governments are usually more determined to balance their budgets than they are to buy off neighborhood opposition to some new public project.

So how should the law set the balance? The current solution aims low by awarding the property owner only the fair market value of the property taken, which is measured at the outset of the project. That rule is correct, insofar as it denies compensation for any increase in property value attributable to the successful completion of the project, which would wrongly assign the social gain from a successful government initiative to an individual owner who did nothing to bring it about. As stated, the fair market value test is meant to provide the "full and perfect equivalent of the property taken." In reality, however, this formula is more restrictive than it looks, because the compensation is measured only with reference to the property taken, ignoring the owner's full losses that are attributable to the taking.

These so-called consequential damages—that is, damages that arise in consequence of the taking—loom large in many cases. The need to compensate for all damages predates the Constitution. As Blackstone said, in takings cases the government protects the owner "by giving him a full indemnification and equivalent for the injury thereby sustained," which can exceed the value of the property taken. Omitting these losses from the compensation formula is a major weakness of modern American takings law. To see why, return again to the basic theory of the takings clause. Recall that legitimate forms of state coercion facilitate the completion of public projects that generate systematic social improvements, without forcing the persons whose property is taken to bear the brunt of the social initiative. That goal is achievable only if the compensation supplied leaves all property owners *in-*

different between property surrendered and the cash or other benefits they receive in exchange. Thereafter, the owners can also share in the social gains—at least so long as they remain in the community.

The fair market value test falls short of meeting this standard on multiple grounds. Start with the simple observation that not every piece of real estate has a "for sale" sign in the window. That point brings to the fore the economic distinction between "use value" and "exchange value." "Use value" is the distinctive subjective value an owner attaches to holding and using property; "exchange value" is the amount an owner expects to realize from selling property, net of the costs of sale. Typically, property's use value exceeds its sale value, so the property remains off the market, usually for reasons of convenience and sentiment. Some businesses want to stay close to their suppliers or customers; homeowners might want to keep close to school and work. People with long-term expectations often customize their property in ways that benefit themselves, but are of little value to anyone else.

The fair market value test *never* reflects that greater use value, and thus systematically undercompensates virtually all property owners. The case law justifies this low-ball estimate by conceding the *existence* of use value but by denying that it can be accurately *measured*. The critics are right to say that it would be foolhardy to take the self-serving testimony of owners at face value. Better too low than too high, goes their standard refrain. But it is possible to pay a fixed "bonus" (say, 10 or 20 percent over market) to compensate use value, without accepting individual evidence. This bonus might be inaccurate in an individual case, but any errors are likely to average out over the long run. Perfect compensation cannot be awarded to each owner, but the overall burdens on the state will better reflect the full cost of its actions and thus help curb excessive condemnations.

In addition to ignoring subjective value, current law also systematically disregards the many costs attendant on the forced dislocation. Valuation procedures in eminent domain cases are costly undertakings. Practically, the law requires every owner to spend money in self-defense, but government awards do not cover reasonable appraisal or legal fees. These costs are not part of the "property taken," but they are, under the parity principle, consequential damages of the state taking. Forcing an individual to bear these costs necessarily reduces his bargaining leverage in negotiations with the state, which has a strong incentive to lowball its compensation offer. Yet the result is often shortsighted, because the low levels of compensation induce major political intrigue as potential condemnees seek to stop or redirect government projects.

Other real losses also receive short shrift in the compensation calculus. Suppose a condemned business has developed goodwill in its present location, which cannot be transferred to another site. Under current law, the government does not need to pay compensation for the goodwill lost because it is not treated as part of the property taken for public use. Yet the same owner could recover for lost goodwill if any private party burned down its store. The parity principle dictates compensation for the destruction of goodwill. Only a concern for the public purse, not the soundness of the takings regime, leads to the opposite result.

Next, suppose a summer camp is ordered to vacate, and must forfeit a grandfathered operating license tied to its present location. The present law does not provide compensation for either the cost of the new license or the loss of interim revenues. Compensation is keyed to the fair market value of the land, and not the owner's replacement cost to reopen the business. Similarly, a displaced pharmacist whose medicines must by law be reopened and reinspected before they can be sold from a different site recovers nothing for their lost value, even if the reinspection costs exceed the value of the medicines inspected. Yet again these losses are not included in just compensation.

PARTIAL CONDEMNATIONS

The situation is even more complex when the taking in question is the taking of a partial interest in real estate. The government may occupy an office for an indefinite term, for example, so long as the war shall continue. Or it may take only part of a plot of land, say for a highway, leaving the owner in possession of the rest. In both cases, it is incorrect to value the loss from property taken in isolation from any change in value to the retained property. Suppose that two acres of land make up a building plot worth $10,000, but the half retained after condemnation is too small for building. The proper compensation is not half of $10,000, or $5,000, but the original $10,000 less the value of the retained land, say $1,000, or $9,000. Likewise, if the government leases land for an indefinite number of years, the reduction in value of the retained interest should be compensable, even if the law is generally otherwise. But sometimes the courts do call a halt. In one situation, the government forced a landlord on little notice to extend its lease on the ground floor of a building. That decision forced the landlord to suspend its scheduled asbestos abatement project for the entire twenty-story structure. Even though the government only took the first floor, it had to pay for the loss of use of the remainder. The loss to the owner, not the gain to the government, is the proper measure of compensation.

Conversely, if government action increases the value of the retained land, that increase is offset against any compensation owing. Historically, for example, highways were so valuable that farmers offered the government land free of charge in order to gain access to markets. For both plusses and minuses, the correct formula sets compensation to leave the property owner indifferent between the property rights taken and the money received.

This formula also covers the holdout problems typical of network industries. Recall the Supreme Court ordered the state to compensate Jean Loretto for attaching a cable box to her apartment house. But how much? The New York court awarded her a dollar for the trivial cost of the actual occupation of roof space. A more accurate measure compensates her for the inability to collect from the cable company the standard industry rental equal to 5 percent of its revenues for gaining access to her tenants. That tiny award looks wrong, especially in New York's rent control environment. The standardized rental agreement removed all holdout problems. Why then should the state intervene in the absence of market failure? The situation is a good case to apply the general rule that governs awards of cash compensation: require the state compensation to leave the landowner as well off when property is taken as before.

Part III Regulatory Takings

CHAPTER SIX

. . .

A Matching Principle
for Regulatory Takings

PAIRING BENEFITS AND BURDENS

Physical takings constitute only the first half of the takings problem. The second half covers regulatory takings. Conceptually, the line between these two classes of takings is drawn as follows. A physical taking deprives an owner of the present or future occupation of his property. A regulatory taking leaves an owner's right to the possession of his property untouched, but restricts his ability to use or dispose of it, or both. The examination of two regimes follows a familiar path. First, do the state restrictions constitute a taking? If not, then the inquiry is at an end. If so, then, second, are the restrictions justified under the state police power? If yes, then no compensation is owed. If no, then, third, are the takings for a public use? If not, then the state action should be blocked or undone to restore the status quo ante. If so, then, fourth, what compensation is required?

All four elements weave their way through the current case law. But although the notes are all there, the melody is discordant.

Today's dominant judicial posture confers great deference to legislators and planners, so that few land use regulations—typically, only those that cause complete economic wipe-out to one or a small group of owners—are compensable under the takings clause. Many of these regulations even eventually receive full judicial blessing under an expansive account of the police power, which courts now reconstrue to encompass any "legitimate state interest" that gains the endorsement of elected political bodies and their expert planners. Today's one-two punch that marries a narrow definition of takings to a broad conception of the police power doctrine seals off virtually all forms of zoning and environmental regulations from judicial challenge. In chapter 8, I will discuss this approach to land use regulation, which dates from the 1926 Supreme Court decision in *Village of Euclid v. Ambler Realty Co.* This chapter explores the weaknesses of the current deferential approach that dominates the judicial landscape.

The first argument in favor of judicial deference is textual. In its ordinary sense, the term "taking" requires dispossession of property, so nothing less will do. That position has some historical support, although the evidence on the question is decidedly mixed on whether, prior to the twentieth century, the takings clause applied to various forms of land use regulation. Nonetheless, the categorical refusal to compensate regulatory takings has been rejected even by writers who think that the historical and textual evidence confines the takings clause to physical occupations. The decisive counterexample is a regulation that denies a single owner any entry or use of his land, without taking away his right to exclude others. Everyone agrees that compensation must be paid. But the class of regulatory takings cannot be so limited. Suppose the state takes a plot of land worth $10,000 from owner A and gives him in exchange an identical plot subject to legal restrictions on use that render it worthless. Surely this counts as a physical taking, without just (indeed, any) compensation. What difference could it make if the state skips the exchange of the two tracts and just imposes the restrictions directly on A's land? The new maneuver allows the state to take an extensive restrictive covenant for free. Surely, courts should invoke the anticircumvention principle to stop this abuse, for nothing in principle requires or allows for the artificial separation of occupation from land use regulation, when both wipe out A's value in his land.

If one landowner can challenge one use restriction under the takings clause, then why not two, or more? The modern embrace of judicial deference evades but does not answer this question. Rather, this outsized deference frequently invites government abuse, especially at the local level. It is therefore vital to outline the alternative framework to explain why and how today's current rules badly miss the constitutional mark. The fundamental analytical tools for understanding regulatory takings have already been deployed to explain physical takings. In the regulatory context as well, the law cannot erect an iron wall between restrictions directed toward a single person and those directed toward many people. The principles used to deal with overflights and rent control easily carry over to regulatory takings. In both areas, the central analytical inquiry asks whether the pattern of benefits generated by the government matches its dislocations, be they large or small. If it does, the measure is constitutional. If not, then it is prima facie unconstitutional.

To see the parallels, first focus on the compensation issues, putting aside any police power justification. If the full brunt of the government action is borne by a single individual, then cash compensation to offset that loss will normally be required, save in the improbable circumstance that the sole beneficiary of the action is the regulated party. Compensation is manifestly required when the government takes the land of just one landowner for a public project. The analysis does not shift when the government engages in "spot zoning," whereby only one landowner is prohibited from building on a single parcel of land. In that case, the owner's loss from government regulation equals one, while the implicit benefits derived are shared with everyone else. In a community of one thousand people, his fractional thousandth of the gain, equal to that of others, never supplies the compensation owing. This imbalanced regulation creates exactly the same political risk as the government occupation, namely, that a majority faction captures all the benefits from that restriction for itself, while forcing its burdens on a single isolated person who lacks political clout.

The analysis then runs through all sorts of intermediate cases where first two or ten people are subject to burdens from which one thousand people benefit. The major challenge comes with regulations that supply matching benefits and burdens to all parties. In these cases, the presumption now shifts, even if the court cannot make a direct valuation of those benefits and burdens. Presumptively, the regulation is imposed because voluntary solutions are not possible with so many interested players. Usually, political safeguards function well because the regulation in its own terms does not isolate any one person or small group.

DISPARATE TREATMENT VERSUS DISPARATE IMPACT

Yet even here, it is critical to factor into the analysis the distinction between disparate *treatment* and disparate *impact*. Disparate treatment is ruled out when a general rule imposes benefits and burdens on the identical set of landowners. Its absence is a

welcome sign that the political system has not worked a redistri-
bution of wealth by taking interests in property from one group
and giving them to another. Singling out particular persons by
name for special consideration is, however, usually a sign of deep
trouble, because that power of selection frees the state of the
troublesome constraint of finding some neutral regulation that
actually does its bidding.

Nonetheless, the converse does not hold. Formal equality does
not necessarily insulate any regulation from a takings challenge,
because it does not exclude the possibility that a regulation that is
neutral on its face will in fact have, perhaps by design, a disparate
impact on two different classes of landowners who are subject to
its command. Here is an example of how it works. A new regulation prohibits all owners in a given area from building any *new*
structures, with no formal distinctions. However, every landowner
except one in the designated area already has built a single-family
home. The last buildable lot must now lie vacant. The formal
parity of the regulation offers no protection to that last owner
against the risk of exploitation. One person is wiped out. All others
are benefited. It is easy to construct numerical examples that show
the point. Let nine lots be arrayed on a tic-tac-toe board, with the
center square vacant. Now impose the prohibition against new
construction. The value of the outside lots will increase by $1,000
each if the restriction is imposed on all lots equally. The central
lot in turn loses $16,000 in value. If the restriction is put to a vote,
it will be approved, with the support of all eight owners of the
outside lots, notwithstanding the $8,000 net loss ($16,000 minus
$8,000) it produces. But if the eight outside owners were forced to
pay $2,000 each to bring the owner of the center lot back to his
preregulatory position, the project would never go through. The
situation looks like this:

+$1,000	+$1,000	+$1,000
+$1,000	−$16,000	+$1,000
+$1,000	+$1,000	+$1,000

Total net losses = $8,000; Vote 8 to 1 in favor

Nor are examples of the dangers of voting in disparate impact cases limited to cases of a single isolated owner. Similar examples can easily be constructed to deal with cases where, for example, on a four-by-three grid, the two central owners suffer greater losses than the ten owners on the periphery by $6,000.

+$1,000	+$1,000	+$1,000	+$1,000
+$1,000	−$8,000	−$8,000	+$1,000
+$1,000	+$1,000	+$1,000	+$1,000

Total net losses = $6,000; Vote 10 to 2 in favor

These dangers are largely obviated when all parties subject to the same regulation are similarly situated. To revert to the initial example, suppose all owners have already built their single-family homes. In these cases, the political process is more likely to work as it should, so that faction and egoism pose smaller obstacles to sound social regulation. As before, each person will vote to maximize private gain over private cost. With identical fractions of benefit and burden, however, no selfish landowner has any incentive to behave in an antisocial way. Thus suppose that the nine landowners on the tic-tac-toe board must decide whether to limit new extensions. If each thinks that the regulation will increase the value of his lot by over $2,000, then he will vote for it, without worrying whether it helps or hurts the others. The unproblematic grid looks like this:

+$2,000	+$2,000	+$2,000
+$2,000	+$2,000	+$2,000
+$2,000	+$2,000	+$2,000

Total net gains = $18,000; Vote 9 to 0 in favor

The only source of conflict in these cases depends on different estimations of the probable effect of the restriction: some owners think that they will reduce the value of all plots, while others think the opposite. At this point, the measure is, necessarily, closely contested. But public deliberation over whether this new restriction will produce a net social gain is a far cry from deliberation by eight landowners in order to wipe out the ninth. On any ordinance with proportionate impact, each owner will seek to persuade others that he has the best judgment on the proposed ordinance. Yet the deliberative strategy for any ordinance with formal equality but with known disparate impact is for the landowners in the majority to forge a winning political coalition that takes advantage of the isolated party. Strong property rights are often put in opposition to deliberative democracy. These examples show that the precise opposite is true. Weak property rights increase the risk of irresponsible public deliberation. Why? Because deliberation in our first example brings together the eight individuals to vote the restriction in place—or to threaten its passage in an effort to extract some advantage from the ninth (a topic to which I shall return in chapter 10).

These oversimplified examples still cry out for a note of caution, for some subtle differences in initial position might justify the explicit form of discrimination. The construction of one home might be on an unstable site that holds out risks for others. But subject to this caveat, the basic position can be summed up as follows. Differential regulation always raises red flags, but formal equality offers no automatic safe harbor for land use regulations. The ultimate message is sobering. In no case can principled courts find any convenient shortcut that allows them to avoid a detailed person-by-person and parcel-by-parcel analysis to determine the net impact of any state restriction. The task is identical to the physical occupation cases, even if the results could play out differently with different regulatory schemes.

Armed with this analysis, the fourfold inquiry into takings sets up an orderly progression for any and all schemes. These various elements are heavily intertwined, and for purposes of exposition, it is often best to see how they operate in tandem. Accordingly, chapters 7–10 compare this analytical approach with the current deferential approach in some of the landmark Supreme Court land use regulation cases. It is not a pretty picture.

CHAPTER SEVEN

Going Too Far

Mineral Rights

SURFACE AND MINERAL INTERESTS

The first of the landmark twentieth-century cases, the 1923 decision in *Pennsylvania Coal Co. v. Mahon*, arose from a prosaic dispute over the mineral rights to anthracite coal in western Pennsylvania. Recall that under the common-law *ad inferos* (to the depths) rule, a surface owner holds exclusive rights to coal (or any other mineral) located beneath his land. But surface and mining activities take place on different scales when a massive coal field lies below land that is dotted with small houses and farms. To increase coal production, surface owners commonly sell or lease their mineral rights to companies that can effectively work the field as a unified whole. When drafting mineral leases, parties must decide who will bear the risk of subsidence, that is, the risk of the surface falling into the ground when the coal is worked out below. Where the miner is under a duty to make sure that the surface is intact, then the surface owner is said to have a right of support, or to own the "support estate." A surface owner who is

The Taft Court. Sitting, left to right: McReynolds, Holmes, Taft, Van Devanter, Brandeis. Standing, left to right: Sanford, Sutherland, Butler, Stone. The Collection of the Supreme Court of the United States.

desirous of having support can accept a lower royalty for the coal from the mine owner, who now bears the risk of loss. Or the surface owner can surrender the right to support in exchange for the receipt of a higher royalty. In these long-term deals, the allocation of this "support estate" applies not only to the original parties but also, on both sides, to their successors in title—that is, anyone who after the initial deal buys either the surface land or the mineral interests.

In the 1870s, several Pennsylvania landowners signed mineral leases that allocated the so-called support estate away to the mine owners. Typically, the mining firms did not aggressively assert their full legal rights to wreck the houses, for the owners of many homes on the surface were also employees in the mines. But one or two mining companies didn't play by the usual rules. In response to complaints, Pennsylvania passed the Kohler Act, which returned the support estate to surface owners, without giving the mining companies any compensation for their loss of rights. The Pennsylvania Coal Company challenged the Act on the ground that it transferred the support estate to the surface owners without just compensation.

GOING "TOO FAR"

The simplest way to view this case is as a transfer of a partial interest in real property from A to B. Justice Oliver Wendell Holmes got to a sound result, but by the wrong path. He first noted, rightly, that the business of government could never go on if each change in the general law was treated as a compensable taking. He then switched gears to hold that the government had to pay compensation when its regulation went "too far," thus plunging the law of regulatory takings into intellectual incoherence, from which it has never escaped. By phrasing the question in this form, he treats everything as a matter of degree, implicitly rejecting all principled distinctions in kind. He would have done far better to address systematically the four key questions in any takings case (listed at the beginning of chapter 6). For starters, did the statute take property from A and give it to B? Holmes hinted that it did by observing that making "it commercially impracticable to mine certain coal has very nearly the same effect for constitutional purposes as appropriating or destroying it." The simpler way of stating the point was that the regulation transferred an interest in property, the support estate, from the mine owners to the surface owners. That counts as a taking of private property for which compensation is prima facie owed.

POLICE POWER AND ASSUMPTION OF RISK

A *Matter of Ends*

The next question asks whether this taking was justified under the police power, in order to protect the property interests of the surface owners. At this point, the parity principle directs us to a critical distinction in the private law. The first question goes to the matter of *ends*. On this question, the police power allows the state to step in, without paying compensation, to protect all individuals from the infliction of ordinary wrongs, including aggression, nuisance, and subsidence. The theory of the power is that the state can act for the benefit of individuals who are unable to coordinate their activities to protect themselves. Put otherwise, if any given individual could have obtained a private injunction for this type of harm without compensating the defendant, then the state can get that injunction for him and others similarly situated, also without compensation. There is here no risk of parties shifting from private or public enforcement to take advantage of a more favorable set of rules. Hence in the context of *Mahon*, the critical question is whether this regulation protected only persons who had assumed a risk by contract with the mine owner or also extended to *strangers*.

In the assumption of risk case, the police power should not be invoked to protect people who have waived their rights just because now they seek public assistance to gain the advantage of more favorable rules. The narrow definition of the police power limits this kind of political arbitrage between markets. But it is important to note the limits of this principle. Thus governments often announce today certain restrictions on building that they plan to impose tomorrow. The government recognizes that the present landowner is not bound by the regulation, but it insists that any future taker of the land, with knowledge of the restriction, is bound, because that buyer has assumed the regulatory risk against which he can guard by paying a lower price.

That analysis is wrong. To say that the buyer takes subject to the risk means that the present owner has to accept a discount in price or keep the property, even when it is more valuable to the buyer. Yet what social gain comes from blocking the free movement of property solely to preserve rights against the government? The better approach follows an automatic rule that allows the present owner to assign his property along with any of his rights to challenge the regulation. That approach both keeps property in commerce and prevents the government from always getting its way by imposing its regulations long in advance of their actual use.

Mahon did not involve the use of any such impermissible government strategy. In that case, the purpose of the regulation was only to allow the surface owners to overcome their coordination problems, not to gain new rights in the public sector. Consistent with this view, the surface owners should have been allowed to set aside these deeds if the mining company engaged in some sharp practice, of which there was no evidence here. But we should be leery of any public policy rule that treats the transfer of the support estate as null and void from its inception. That rule has the unfortunate effect of forcing the parties to choose between two unpalatable alternatives: conveying the surface to the mining company that doesn't need it, or forgoing any deal at all. Both of these are vastly inferior to the split ownership solution adopted. In these property transactions, therefore, any police power claim should be trumped by conveyances that have explicitly taken the risk into account, as all well-drawn leases do. Accordingly, the state regulation in *Mahon* falls outside the police power.

The stranger cases require a different analysis. Now the police power addresses legitimate ends, because the regulation protects people against future harms (such as subsidence) that they could privately enjoin since they have not waived their rights by contract. Their difficulty, of course, is figuring out how to organize their joint activities, which is very difficult to do when many people each have a small stake in the overall venture. At this point, the use of a regulatory solution overcomes the coordination problems separate surface owners face, by using the state as an agent that allows separate persons to act as one in order to stop the harm in question. Since these landowners were entitled, but unable, to bring suit, before the regulation was passed, the state action on their behalf is wholly proper, for direct public enforcement does not give them any advantages that they were not entitled to under the private law. The case does not allow individuals who were remediless under the private law to secure illicit gains by shifting to the public forum to obtain relief that was otherwise wholly unavailable as a matter of right.

A Matter of Means

Once the ends are legitimate, the question arises of *means* both for private injunctions and direct public regulation. When a particular harm is certain to occur, it is surely correct to stop the activity before any harm happens. It is, however, commonly uncertain whether the mines would cave in without the support. At this point, the law has to come to grips with two kinds of error in deciding whether to issue injunctive relief. Type 1 error arises when the state imposes the regulation only to discover after the fact that it was unnecessary to stop the harm. Conversely, type 2 error arises where the state allows an action to go forward that does cause avoidable harm.

Constitutional law must assign relative weights to these two forms of error. A standard of *strict scrutiny* weights type 1 error much more heavily than type 2 error, so very few government actions pass muster. That standard might work for government censorship, but it is too strict here. At the opposite extreme, the *rational basis* test weighs type 2 error much more heavily than type 1 error, so that very few government regulations are struck down. This test is in all likelihood too lenient, given that private damage actions still supply a strong deterrent effect, even if the injunction is denied.

On balance, therefore, the sensible approach is to weigh both types of error about equally, under a standard of *intermediate scrutiny*. So long as there is a reasonable probability that the regulation is necessary to stop the harm to strangers, it should be allowed. If the Kohler Act passes muster on ends, then it probably passes muster on means as well. Or more cautiously, the mine owner should have to explain why these particular government restrictions did not serve to advance health and safety, but in fact crippled the activity of the regulated mine solely to advance the competitive position of its rivals. That case looks hard to make out. Today, however, the rational basis test removes the need for that kind of showing. We therefore get lots of regulation of limited social value. Yet as matters stand, it would take a major, if welcome, revolution to get courts to weigh the two types of error equally.

JUST COMPENSATION AGAIN

On the third question, we can assume that this taking meets the public use test, if only because the coordination problems make it hard for any voluntary transaction to reassign the support rights to the surface owners, given that such a reassignment makes business sense only if *all* surface owners participate. Otherwise, some surface owners will be able to free-ride on the others, for once the mine owner alters its operations to avoid subsidence to some surface owners, it protects all surface owners. The Kohler Act was rightly held unconstitutional because it forced a switch in property rights without offering the mine owners just compensation. But suppose compensation was offered—what should be its measure, and who should pay it? Need compensation be paid only for the coal left in place—that is, "the" property taken by the statute—or must it cover all consequential damages, including the increased cost of operating the mine? The latter, of course, is the correct measure, given that the purpose of compensation is to return the regulated mine owners to their prestatutory level of wealth. The basic analysis, moreover, highlights the tenuous distinction between a taking and a "mere" regulation. Consider these two statutory schemes. First, Pennsylvania allows the mine companies to remove all the coal so long as they shore up the surface. There is no requirement that any coal be left in place. Without doubt, this law would be classified as a regulation, which would pass constitutional muster because of the low standard of review applied to regulatory takings. Second, in the alternative, Pennsylvania requires that the support be maintained by keeping pillars of coal in place. Now there is a physical taking subject to a high standard of review, which would flunk constitutional muster in virtually all cases. But wherein lies the difference?—for nothing would have changed if the Kohler Act had not required the mine owners to leave coal in place, but instead let them shore up the surface with artificial supports. The small difference between the two legal regimes should never generate such dramatic consequences. Compensation is appropriate in both cases for the diminution in value worked by the statutory scheme.

Finally, who should pay the required just compensation? In this instance, it seems odd to take the money out of general revenues when only a discrete class of landowners has its houses propped up. Once again, the matching principle supplies the right answer. In principle, the payments should be paid by a *special* assessment, levied against only the homes that receive the support easement, in proportion to their value. This focused imposition has the added benefit of preventing the usual forms of political lobbying that pop up when these landowners can use *other* people's tax dollars to pay for their own private benefit. This system would also avoid the holdout problem among surface owners by stipulating a unique allocation of loss.

The special assessment regime has one obvious weakness that can be easily remedied. How do we determine whether the surface owners value, on average, the support easement more than their costs of acquiring it? The best way to obtain this information is to run a minielection, often by supermajority vote of surface owners, measured by the value of their lands, to decide whether it makes sense to go forward with the project at all. This approach works well here because the distribution of benefits and burdens satisfies the matching principle set out in the previous chapter. Yet in other contexts it will fail. Local residents will resist a special assessment for a road that primarily serves through traffic. Special assessments will also founder if the voting area includes individuals who are bound by the decision but get no part of the benefit. The worst offender on this score was Justice Holmes, who upheld a special assessment that charged the property owners on both sides of a new road for the costs of its construction. One side owned a railroad that ran parallel to the road and would hardly benefit from a road to which it had no access and from which it received competition for passengers and commercial traffic. Yet another casualty of the rational basis test.

Unfortunately, Justice Holmes never broached the overall question of system design in *Mahon*, because the Kohler Act did not offer any compensation. But by making compensability turn on a regulation's going "too far," he darkened takings law to the present day. In general, any decision on whether a private defendant should be liable in tort or whether the government should be liable for a taking should be hard-edged. All liability questions demand yes-or-no answers that are best attained by bright-line rules. Was the ball fair or foul? Did the defendant drive his car across the middle of the road? Did the Kohler Act undo the original grant? If it did, then compensation follows to the extent of the loss. If not, then none is needed. Holmes's "too far" question turns a bright-line question into a matter of degree for no good reason. "Too far" answers the question *how much* is owed, not *whether anything* is owed at all. When regulatory takings are governed by Holmes's test, small matters of degree generate immense distinctions in kind. But deciding where to draw the line between takings and mere regulations is, as we shall see, a far easier question to pose than to answer.

CHAPTER EIGHT

Adventures in Land Use Regulation

Zoning and Landmark Preservation

EUCLID AND THE RISE OF LAND USE PLANNING

The intellectual confusion sowed by the Holmes formula quickly shaped the zoning cases that came down shortly after *Mahon*. Zoning was a relatively new and untested American innovation in the first part of the twentieth century. It first surfaced as a major Progressive innovation in New York City in 1916, spurred on by the spread of the garment industry into fashionable Fifth Avenue neighborhoods and by the desire to limit the height of new skyscrapers. Zoning laws got a further boost when the United States Department of Commerce under Herbert Hoover promulgated the Standard State Zoning Enabling Act in 1926. The bipartisan motives of economic and aesthetic protection were present at the creation. So, too, was the Progressive faith in science and technical expertise that fueled the rise of the administrative state. Zoning law called for local planning boards to divide city territories into different zones—manufacturing, commercial, and various kinds of residential—so as to minimize harmful interactions between

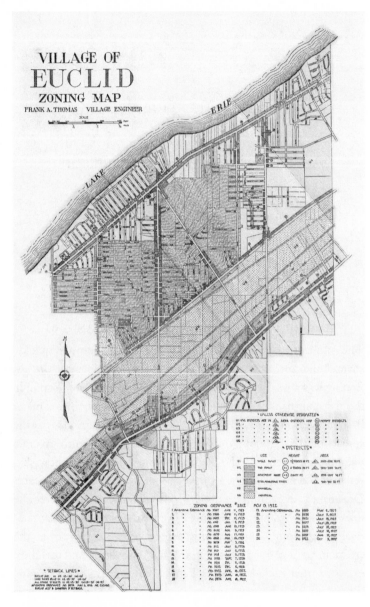

Village of Euclid Zoning Map. Courtesy Euclid Historical Society.

neighbors. Whether this separation makes sense for most communities is hotly debated to this day, for many writers follow the late Jane Jacobs in thinking that mixed uses do more than sterile single-use zones to create a sense of community and excitement.

The Supreme Court faced its first zoning challenge in the epic 1926 case of *Euclid v. Ambler Realty Company*. Ambler Realty owned a compact 68-acre plot of land bordering the Nickel Plate Railroad on the north. The firm wanted to develop the tract into an industrial site for a Fisher Body plant. A local ordinance broke that tract into three different zones, the northernmost for manufacturing, the middle one for apartment houses, and the southern one for single- and two-family homes. So divided, the zoned property lost around 75 percent of its market value, declining roughly from $800,000 to $200,000. Did these use restrictions constitute a taking requiring just compensation?

Justice Sutherland's decision did not concentrate much on how this particular ordinance operated, but instead addressed in sweeping terms the urban evils that zoning was intended to combat. These included everything from contagion and fire to keeping "apartment parasites" (yes, there were clear racial overtones here) from preying on single-family homes. The upshot was that he showed great deference to local planning, so long as the property retained some value for development, as it surely did in this case. In particular, he held that the police power was not confined to its traditional role of stopping nuisances, but was capacious enough to include any systematic effort to improve the overall condition of the community. He then upheld the ordinance. The three dissenting judges filed no opinion.

TWO VIEWS ON LAND USE RESTRICTIONS

It is best to examine *Euclid* through the lens of our four familiar questions (listed at the beginning of chapter 6). First, the village imposed a large restrictive covenant on the use of Ambler's parcel, diminishing its value. This action counts prima facie as a compensable taking under the parity principle. Neighbors could never have imposed these restrictions on Ambler. Nor does it matter at this stage that the ordinance may have taken similar use rights in property from other owners. The prima facie case of A remains, even if B's land is subject to an identical restriction.

Second, any assessment of the police power justification for this ordinance requires looking not at zoning laws in general, but at their particular impact on this tract of land. Building this factory, set back from the boundary line, would not have come within a country mile of an ordinary nuisance. But if the factory, once running, ever became a nuisance because of its impact on its neighbors, *at that time* they could enjoin its operation under the familiar common-law principles that properly give little if any weight to the hardship the injunction works on the defendant's operations. The tough prospect prevents landowners from stepping out of line. Third, we can assume that the zoning regulation has some legitimate public use in mind, for its aesthetic gains are not confined to some narrow group. So it all comes down to just compensation. And it is here where the ordinance fails. Few local governments would adopt this ordinance if it carried a hefty price tag.

Many modern writers in the progressive tradition think that any judicial overriding of the experts is reason enough to condemn this approach to takings. But that skepticism is misplaced from a social point of view. In *Euclid*, it is unquestionable that Ambler lost roughly $600,000 in value. Where is $600,000 worth of benefits to others? Of course, some neighbors would have preferred that the factory not be built in their backyards, which explains the durability of the NIMBY (Not-In-My-Back-Yard) movement. But other neighbors, seeking either employment or business, might covet a new plant in their backyards. All these soft aesthetic and social effects, both positive and negative, form part of the grand social calculus, even in the absence of any common-law nuisance. But any analysis proceeds down a two-way street. It is *not* proper to consider only those diffuse social harms that the zoning regulation prevents without considering the social benefits it simultaneously blocks. On balance, these are likely to cancel out, in which case Ambler's loss now is a reasonable proxy for the *net* social loss caused by the regulation. Ignoring its "private" loss is thus a profoundly *asocial* position. If by chance, the diffuse social gains do outweigh the localized costs, then the "winners" should be able to push the condemnation measure through, *with compensation.* The nub of the danger is this: without question, under *Euclid*'s no-compensation rule, majorities that value the factory's removal by less than Ambler's loss—say $200,000—could prevail in local electoral politics, notwithstanding the net $400,000 losses in property values they impose (to which must be added the costs of advancing and resisting their initiative). Why adopt legal arrangements that foster large losses for small gains?

LANDMARK PRESERVATION STATUTES

The consequences of *Euclid* reverberate to this day. Indeed, with a few minor exceptions, *Euclid*'s Progressive-era zoning regime received no serious challenge until the Penn Central Company claimed that New York's landmark preservation ordinance was a taking of its air rights over Grand Central Station. New York's Landmarks Commission blocked Penn Central's construction of a fancy fifty-five-story Breuer tower that met all local zoning ordinances. By designating the site "protected," it vetoed a project that would have generated well over $2 million in annual net rentals to Penn Central. The capitalized value of that rental stream represents a *low* estimate of the social loss inflicted by the landmark designation program, because that figure ignores the gains to Penn Central's tenants from using the proposed building. Yet, as with *Euclid*, *Penn Central* raises the difficult aesthetic question of whether this tower should count as the creation of a new landmark or the desecration of an old one. (After all, some of the truly memorable buildings we take pride in today would never have been built if preservation statutes had been in place when they were constructed.) And in contrast to *Euclid*, the commission offered what are commonly called "transferable development rights" (TDRs), which gave Penn Central the right to use designated air rights over someone else's land, but only with their consent, and only if it met all the permitting conditions of the new site. These TDRs do have value, and are sometimes bought and sold. By no stretch of the imagination are they a full and perfect equivalent of the original air rights.

Notwithstanding these evident difficulties, in the case of *Penn Central v. City of New York*, Justice Brennan rebuffed all takings challenges to the ordinance. First, he said that he was loath to strike down preservation techniques that had been adopted in every state. Second, he rejected the disproportionate impact formula developed in the *Armstrong* case (see chapter 3), which would require compensation. In his view, all takings cases had to be decided by "ad hoc inquiries," rather than by clear principles. His approach led to a three-part balancing test that exerts immense influence today. First, consider the nature of the taking—landowners in physical takings receive more protection than in regulatory ones. Next, consider the extent of the state's interest in preservation. Third, with shades of Holmes, consider the extent of the owner's loss attributable to the regulation. To Brennan, the takings inquiry ultimately turns on whether the statute frustrates some set of "investment-backed expectations" of the "single parcel" considered as a whole.

Marcel Breuer's plan for a building on top of Grand Central Station,
1968. Courtesy Marcel Breuer Papers, Archives of American Art,
Smithsonian Institution.

Using this approach, he stressed that New York City's landmark preservation ordinance is a regulation of future development rights that leaves all existing uses untouched. He then concluded that the strong social interest in neighborhood preservation justified the ordinance. The TDRs helped sustain the law, because they gave the owner some compensation for the loss of the air rights. Justice Rehnquist's dissent avoided a frontal assault on *Euclid* by rejecting this ordinance as an invidious form of "spot zoning." As that term suggests (in light of the tic-tac-toe grid example in chapter 6), he believed that zoning laws should be subject to additional scrutiny when they pick out a single or very few owners—or "spot"—to which the regulation only applies. To Rehnquist, the scheme failed because it lacked even the sign of formal equality across landowners.

The Rehnquist approach yields, at least in this case, the right result. Brennan's ad hoc approach is flatly inconsistent with the results of our familiar four-fold inquiry. First, under the *ad coelum* doctrine, air rights have long been recognized as property interests that an owner can use, sell, mortgage or lease. They represent a divided interest in property that is taken when the state prohibits the owner from using them at all. The parallel to the coal-left-in-place in *Pennsylvania Coal* is precise. The government has taken Penn Central's air rights, whether it mothballs them or sells them or gives them to a third party—as TDRs, no less—which it can do only by first claiming to own them. Second, Brennan cannot point to any nuisance to justify stopping the construction of this tower, especially when the building of other structures is allowed, including the huge Pan Am tower just to the north of Grand Central Station.

Third, the public use test is easily satisfied in this case, so that the just compensation issue becomes critical. Here the assigned TDRs did not come close to covering the lost value. As in *Euclid*, it is far better to have a single place to build now than a set of fragmented rights to build, perhaps tomorrow, somewhere else. Worse still, using this device sets up a dangerous dynamic of letting the state pay compensation with funny money that is by design hard to value. It is far better to preserve transparency in public business by avoiding this disguised form of barter. The government should pay cold cash for what it takes, and sell any TDRs it has in competitive markets, with honest valuations. Rehnquist's dissent rightly rejected Brennan's ad hoc approach, but wrongly shied away from any attack on *Euclid*.

INVESTMENT-BACKED EXPECTATIONS
AND THE DENOMINATOR PROBLEM

Unfortunately, Brennan's *Penn Central* decision has spawned immense doctrinal confusion. To this day, no one quite knows when, or how, investment-backed expectations attach. Does it make a difference that the air rights are stripped away long before their owner decides to build, or do these expectations only "vest" after a construction project begins? The latter position is generally adopted today. Not surprisingly, it has the unfortunate consequence of hastening development solely to protect future rights to build.

Moreover, no one knows what counts as a "single parcel." This question is critical, because only if "the" property is identified does it become possible to determine whether there is a sufficient loss in property value as Brennan's third factor (and the older *Mahon* test) requires. That determination was easy in *Penn Central* because of its unambiguous history as a single-building site. But in the ensuing years, the lower courts have asked in case after case what happens when sole owners, married couples, extended families, and their trusts, partnerships, and corporations acquire contiguous plots of land in different proportions at different times under different instruments, when some but not all of these parcels are rendered worthless.

Modern scholarship calls this the "denominator" problem. If the so-called denominator—that is, the property regulated—is described as a distinct component of the larger assemblage, then any regulation that renders it worthless counts as a compensable taking. But if the denominator includes all or most of a group of contiguous plots, then even though the absolute value of the loss is unchanged, the *fractional* loss is diminished, so that often no compensation is owed. To revert back to our tic-tac-toe board, assume that all squares are subject to common ownership. If the center square alone is considered "the" property, then any regulation that renders it worthless is compensable. But if all nine squares are considered part of the whole, then the wipeout in the center is of no consequence so long as each of the lots on the periphery retains its value. Thus to return to the example in chapter 6, assume that each of the eight lots on the periphery gains $1,000 while the lot in the center loses all $16,000 in value. The wipeout in the center does not matter on the modern view because of the gains elsewhere. In fact an accurate assessment requires that the $16,000 in compensation be reduced by the gains that the owner obtains elsewhere, but that netting process has no role whatsoever under the *Penn Central* framework.

This stress on the third *Penn Central* factor illustrates the huge gulf that the current law creates between physical occupation and restrictive zoning. In physical occupation cases, the compensation is measured by the loss in value of the property taken: denominators are irrelevant. Take an acre of land, and you pay for an acre of land, no matter what the size of the overall parcel. With regulations, however, the threshold question is whether the fraction in value lost is large enough to require compensation. Now denominators are everything. Both sides respond to the perverse legal incentives: owners try to make bits of land into discrete properties, while local governments seek to aggregate isolated parcels. That entire exercise bears no relationship to the political risks—namely those of faction and majority oppression—that the takings clause is intended to counter. The same rule should apply to both occupations and use restrictions. Once either has occurred, the resulting diminution in property values should be prima facie compensable in both contexts.

THE RUSH TO DESIGNATE

The moral, quite simply, is that any coherent approach requires courts in land use cases to bite off more than most are willing to chew. Rather than act coherently, they prefer to pretend that losses from regulation are cut from the same cloth as those from market competition by state or private firms, even though only the former involve the loss of an interest in real property. Once again, courts violate the parity principle by consciously misstating the private law of damages, to which this longstanding distinction is central. Their cavalier approach insulates state authorities from the harmful consequences of their actions, encouraging them to landmark buildings of dubious merit to stop sensible development that can promote neighborhood growth. My favorite example was the dark-of-night decision by the city of Chicago to designate as a landmark the nondescript American Correspondence School, located in the heart of the University of Chicago campus. The political motivation was to slow down the expansion of the university's hospital for the benefit of nearby neighbors, who opposed the project. These neighbors sold out within a few years anyhow, leaving the university with a markedly inferior facility and an eyesore to boot. Time and again, the officials and citizens who are prepared to *designate* a building as a landmark are unwilling to *buy* it.

In his defense, Justice Brennan was quite right to note in *Penn Central* that public ownership of valuable landmark buildings is an unwise alternative. But regulation by designation is hardly better, for Brennan's observation misses two points. First, oppressive designations often induce private owners to let their property decay. Second, the state, or any private organization, has a *purchase* alternative that Brennan ignored. A sensible local government could buy the property outright and then sell it off to a private owner subject to restrictions that protect its landmarked exterior. Or private parties, such as the Landmark Preservation Council of Illinois (on which I served) can, and do, buy select properties, whether or not designated, on their own account. This is how the Council saved Mies van der Rohe's 1951 Edith Farnsworth House. The Illinois Council acquired the house by entering the market as a purchaser, after which it promptly transferred the property to the National Trust. The options here are perfectly clear. Both private and public parties have the option to buy properties outright and resell subject to terms that restrict their use and preserve their facades. The sale will realize less money than the purchase price, but will allow the preservationists to keep what they hold most dear. In the alternative, the public or private parties could leave the property in the hands of its present owners and purchase a preservation easement that limits what the present owner can do with the exterior of the structure. Both systems allow the preservationists to claim only those interests that they want in the property, freeing the extra cash for use in other acquisitions. The program does not involve any form of confiscation through regulation. If need be, the system of purchase can be supplemented by modest tax subsidies that reflect the benefits that preservation confers on the public at large. The Progressives were wrong: there is no enduring conflict between a system of strong property rights and the advancement of community values.

CHAPTER NINE

The Environmental Challenge

THE *LUCAS* CASE

The fundamental misconceptions behind *Penn Central* have unfortunately proved highly influential in setting the constitutional framework for environmental regulation. In *Lucas v. South Carolina Coastal Council*, David Lucas, a former Clemson University football player, owned two beachfront plots on Palm Island, South Carolina, smack in the middle of hurricane country. Nonetheless, one lot was worth $650,000, and the other had a similar but unstated value—until the South Carolina Coastal Council prohibited him from building anything on either. That ordinance did not single out his property, but applied to all unbuilt sites. The stated justification for the ordinance was that it promoted local tourism by controlling development and maintaining open spaces in their natural condition. But that argument makes the regulation look like a taking for a public use for which compensation is required. As the litigation progressed, the state shifted its ground, arguing that its goal was to prevent harm, by preventing building debris from injuring persons caught on the beach during a storm.

That supposed protection came at a steep price, because the South Carolina ordinance wiped out the value of both plots as building sites. Justice Scalia held that the regulation was tantamount to a compensable physical taking on the ground that it eliminated all economically viable use of the land. On the justification question, Scalia waffled on the proper baseline for analysis: did this ordinance merely "confer a benefit on the public at large" or did it "prevent the landowner from causing harm to others"? His skepticism about the harm/benefit distinction is no small matter. If that line is unintelligible, then so, too, is the line between the police power and public use. At that point the takings clause becomes unglued, because a police power justification allows the state to regulate *without* compensation, while a public use rationale allows for regulation only *with* compensation. It hardly helps to say that the only feasible line is useless, leaving it impossible to tell when private owners are entitled to compensation.

Fortunately, Justice Scalia did not stop with these gauzy ruminations. In the end, he inched back to the parity principle by tying the police power to the common definition of nuisance found in the *Restatement (Second) of Torts*, which contains a distillation of the American common-law rules. Accordingly, whenever a private individual may enjoin certain forms of misconduct— chiefly common-law nuisances—as of right, the state may enjoin as his agent, also without compensation. So, after his prolonged philosophical detour, Scalia concluded that if Lucas's new home had constituted a common-law nuisance, then the state could prohibit its construction under the police power. But since it was not a nuisance, the state either had to back off or pay full value for the property.

Herein lies a tale that exposes the danger of government cheap talk. On remand, the trial judge found that the regulations effectuated a complete taking. To make the transaction official, he ordered Lucas to deed title to the property over to the state, which had to pay for the land in cash, from which Lucas paid off his mortgage. How was the state to raise the hundreds of thousands of dollars necessary to pay for these two plots of vacant land? First, it tried to sell one of them to neighbors, who would pay about 65 percent of the value for gaining a side yard. But that left it over $400,000 short, with one lot to go. So in the end, it sold off the two lots for their market value, *by allowing their new owners to build on the property.* It is easy to trumpet environmental values when you don't have to pay for them. But actual behavior is a better indicator of true public preferences.

TEMPORARY AND PERMANENT TAKINGS

Lucas was in a sense a fluke, because the ordinance unquestionably left the owner with no viable economic use for the sites. But Scalia's temporary fix did not cure the underlying intellectual incoherence. During the litigation, South Carolina amended its regulations to allow the construction of new homes by individuals who were willing to fight their way through onerous restrictions and long delays. But what about the total loss of use during the interim period? In 1987, the Supreme Court held in *First English Evangelical Lutheran Church v. County of Los Angeles* that a "temporary total taking" constituted a compensable event. But in the next breath, the Court backtracked somewhat by allowing the planning agencies a "normal" planning period before deciding whether to issue a permit. Local governments promptly lengthened their review schedules, so that in many cases futile twenty-year review cycles have left frustrated owners with unbuilt lots.

The longer the delays, the greater the risk of being caught by *First English*. Thus a common pattern has emerged whereby federal and state authorities take turns blocking development.

Such interminable litigation exposes the soft underbelly of the Scalia rule. If a total prohibition on using a beachfront lot requires full payment, then the state may shift to partial restrictions on the *Euclid* model, and pay nothing. That evasion disappears if these restrictions are compensable takings unless justified under the nuisance-based view of the police power used in *Lucas*. But once again, Justice Scalia was not prepared to pull the trigger. He concluded that "permanent partial takings" fell under the deferential *Penn Central* rule, which spells curtains for virtually all landowner claims.

POLLUTION AND PRESERVATION

Harms or Benefits

Just how the current law unleashes a powerful one-two punch when it marries a narrow view of government takings to a broad view of its police power is shown by *Lucas*'s narrow victory. The police power issue gains importance as environmentalism surges forward. The common response is that common-law property rules cannot deal with the inconvenient truths of the environmental revolution. At one level, this response is correct. Our greater knowledge of pollutant dispersion through land and water dispels the naïve claim that certain activities, like farming, do not generate negative externalities. But that insight does not require a redefinition of nuisance law that wipes out the harm/benefit distinction. It only requires that we pair up traditional nuisance law with advanced evidentiary techniques that enables us to trace all pollutants to their source. Under the parity principle, private landowners have recourse to the same techniques, to deny any causal connection. The basic rules of private property have a built-in dynamic element.

Much modern environmental law starts with the observation that nuisances come in all sizes and shapes. The private rights of action that allow one landowner to combat a massive spill from his neighbors cannot stop countless instances of tailpipe pollution with widespread negative effects. But this practical difficulty does not require us to junk the older substantive law of nuisance. Rather, it only requires us to adopt legal procedures that are sensitive to scale and administrative costs. When diffuse forms of pollution rise above a tolerable background level, the right response is to abandon private rights of action in favor of other modes of social control. Class actions are one cumbersome alternative. Direct taxes or emissions regulations are likely to prove more efficient. The takings law welcomes any procedural innovation that vindicates the entitlements between neighbors that the common law of nuisance provides. It asks only that the means be proportional to the ends, a requirement that carries over from the common-law rules on damages and injunctions.

The modern environmental movement is not hostile to these maneuvers, but it takes an additional step with radically different implications. It seeks to *expand* the class of environmental wrongs by knocking out the harm/benefit distinction. This tactic has been used both with wetlands and endangered species. Both forms of regulation are for public use, so understanding their operation turns on the interplay of takings, police power, and just compensation issues.

Wetlands

It is widely thought that wetlands serve important ecological functions. They maintain wildlife and the long-term balance of nature. But that proposition does not entitle the Army Corps of Engineers or a state department of natural resources to enjoy the power to issue or deny building or filling permits at will. Under the three-part *Penn Central* test, these regulatory orders have an uncertain fate, because of the constant disputes over whether "the" parcel covers only the targeted wetlands or also includes some adjacent uplands. The environmental interest always receives a high rating. Therefore, under the current law, the negative impact on development will tip the balance toward compensation only when the regulation wipes out all property values, and perhaps not even then. Most states aggressively use their broad power to designate wetlands not only in isolated places with little commercial value but also in tire tracks on vacant city lots. Freeing public bodies from the duty to compensate removes the incentive for environmental groups to recognize the value in alternative property uses or to intelligently determine which wetlands are worth preserving. As with coastlands, governments are all too eager to use wetland designations on lands they would never purchase.

My four-part takings analysis leads to the opposite result. The use restriction counts as a partial taking, just as in the zoning cases. The state, however, can rarely show the need to abate a common-law nuisance under the police power—which includes the traditional public nuisances that arise when landfills discharge waste into public waters. But if the state wants to use private wetlands to *purify* public waters, then it should buy them, just as it would buy uplands for a water purification plant. It is as if the state insisted that owners leave their private land undeveloped for wild animals to graze. The operative distinction is this. No compensation is needed to combat spillovers, literally construed, onto public lands and waters. Full compensation is needed to restrict private use for habitat creation only.

Note the social gains that come from adopting the proper system. In both zoning and environmental settings, the compensation requirement creates the price system that forces the state to examine its priorities. That difference matters. Here is one illustration. The Audubon Society owns extensive wetlands in many sensitive areas. Yet it happily leases these sensitive sites to oil companies, who pay a lower royalty in exchange for taking greater precautions against harm. The Audubon Society uses the royalty payments to buy additional lands to use and lease. Similarly, lumber companies commonly use their forests for other purposes, such as recreational parks and campsites, until the trees are ready for harvest. No state that enjoys the power to designate wetlands ever develops such a system of mixed uses. Yet both the Audubon Society and the lumber company examples provide conclusive evidence that intelligent systems of mixed uses trump single-use designations—and the bitter political struggles that both proceed and follow them.

Endangered Species

The same arguments apply to habitat designation for endangered species. The courts have routinely upheld the power of the federal government to decree that removing privately owned habitat from endangered species is a criminal offense. They view the statutory prohibition against causing "harm" as broad enough to allow the Department of Interior to include habitat destruction within its scope. But even if the statute explicitly equated habitat destruction with killing wild animals, it would still run afoul of the takings clause, because it obliterates the harm/benefit distinction.

Invalidation of such statutes should be welcomed from a social point of view. The expansion of the harm principle converts the discovery of any valuable species on private lands from a source of new wealth to its owner into a mortal threat to the land's productivity. In consequence, the rational landowner now has, as the saying goes, an incentive to shoot, shovel, and shut up. But the owner's incentives change if the state (or any private party) has to buy the habitat rights. Now the landowner's discovery gives him something to sell; shoot, shovel, and shut up becomes a self-destructive strategy. It is far better to preserve the scarce asset for sale. For its part, the state now chooses to buy habitat that it thinks is worth more than it costs. Those transfer payments are neither social gains nor losses. What matters are the signals that a sound price system sends to government officials and landowners alike on how they should behave. The incentives here are wholly different, moreover, from those that would arise if the state were forced to buy out individuals who threatened to commit common-law nuisances. There is a finite supply of habitat, which needs incentives for preservation. In contrast, landowners will find ways to generate an endless supply of nuisances if the state or any private party cannot enjoin them but must be prepared to buy them off. The harm/benefit distinction reflects that key difference in the right set of incentives for dealing with long-term effects. To be sure, recent advances in environmental science raise real management problems, but these changes in technology do not undermine the classical synthesis embodied in the takings clause. Now more than ever, holding fast to the old distinctions creates a sensible system of property rights that no system of state socialism in wildlife can emulate.

CHAPTER TEN

The Exaction Game

UNDOING ZONING?

The previous chapters have demonstrated the systematic social inefficiencies that flow from uncompensated government restrictions on land use. Exhibit A was the zoning ordinance in *Euclid* that reduced the value of an $800,000 piece of property by $600,000. The question is what, if anything, can be done to mitigate that loss. Real possibilities for beneficial exchange arise if, as seems likely, the regulation produced a public gain of, say, $250,000, which is smaller than the loss sustained by the original owner. Once the ordinance takes effect, the system is out of equilibrium, because *both* the village of Euclid and Ambler Realty can be made better off by a second deal in which Ambler pays the village more than $250,000 and less than $600,000 in order to return to the status quo ante.

For ease of exposition, assume that the cost of wrangling is $100,000, which is equally borne. Now a transfer payment of

$425,000 would improve the village's position by $125,000. The calculation runs as follows:

Cash received ($425,000) – lost public amenities ($250,000) – wrangling costs ($50,000) = village gain ($125,000)

Ambler Realty would also improve its net position by $125,000, from $200,000 to $325,000, as follows:

Regained land use ($600,000) – cash paid ($425,000) – wrangling costs ($50,000) = Ambler Realty gain ($125,000)

Together the parties realize $250,000 from the recontracting. Of course, the second deal would have to bind the state not to reimpose the ordinance, which in most places can be done by explicit contract.

This scenario offers us in reality a cautionary tale, for we could generate a further social improvement of at least $100,000 by blocking *both* the initial taking and the subsequent renegotiation. That is a low estimate, because blocking both transactions also removes the costs of securing the ordinance in the first place, which could easily equal those costs incurred to remove it altogether. Quite simply, there is little benefit in taking an entitlement from one party solely for the purpose of resale to its original owner.

The cycle of intrigue, however, expands once *Euclid* is in place. The initial zoning ordinance was adopted solely to change land use patterns. But after the first successful renegotiation, local governments either impose or threaten new zoning ordinances in order to set the stage for an *exaction game*: the ordinance is proposed solely as a threat to induce the landowner to buy his way out of it by offering concessions the government could not otherwise demand as of right. Even courts sympathetic to zoning are understandably queasy about making these threats. Behind their uneasiness lies the clear sense that these threats undermine the matching principle that requires ordinary real estate taxes to fund basic local improvements of equal benefit to current residents and new arrivals.

Local governments run the exaction game by offering to allow landowners to buy their way out of abiding by restrictions by contributing money or land to public purposes. The new deal says that a builder can escape a setback or use restriction by contributing cash to a fund for neighborhood beautification, or by making *in-kind* transfer to the government, for example, by donating land for a public park open to present residents. The landowner capitulates because he is better off with the exaction than he would have been under the restrictions, which were ramped up to provide additional leverage.

SWAPPING EASEMENTS FOR RESTRICTIONS

Surprisingly, this government tactic received its first explicit judicial examination only in 1987, with the Supreme Court's decision in *Nollan v. California Coastal Commission*. The Nollans owned beachfront property on the Pacific Ocean in Ventura County just to the west of the Pacific Coast Highway (PCH). To the north was Faria Beach; to the south lay another beach called "The Cove." The house on the Nollans' parcel was old and dilapidated, worth relatively little, say, $100,000. Building a new home on the site would have increased the value of the property to $500,000, net of the cost of construction. On these numbers, the permit to build was worth $400,000 to the Nollans.

The California Coastal Commission holds extensive powers over new construction along the Pacific Ocean. It claimed the power to impose building restrictions on landowners in order to preserve the ocean views of motorists on the PCH. Flexing its muscle, it proposed the following deal, similar to the one most of the Nollans' neighbors had accepted. The commission would allow the Nollans to build their new house, but only if they deeded over to the commission a lateral easement over the front portion of the land that allowed members of the public to go freely between Faria Beach and The Cove. Assume that easement reduces the value to the Nollans of their land by $100,000, but increases the public value of the beaches by $75,000. At this point, the temptation is irresistible: surrender the public easement. The Coastal Commission improves the position of its citizenry, and the Nollans come out $300,000 ahead. Everyone wins. The Nollans, however, defied the ban, built their new house, and refused to deed over the easement. Justice Scalia held that the win-win trade the Coastal Commission proposed was simply an impermissible form of "out-and-out extortion." The Nollans' house remained standing, and the lateral easement was denied.

To reach this result, Scalia invoked the vexing legal doctrine of unconstitutional conditions: the state may have the right to grant or withhold permission at will, but it cannot grant permission subject to any conditions that threaten the basic constitutional order. A simple example of this principle holds that the state may keep large rigs from the public highways, or allow them to enter. It can surely condition entry onto the highway on the willingness of rig owners to pay vehicle taxes proportionate to the road damage they inflict, or to be sued in state courts for local accidents. By traditional parlance, these conditions are "germane" to the exercise of the state power. Yet it is a different kettle of fish for the state to say that such rigs will be allowed on the public highway only if their owners agree to waive all their rights against unreasonable searches and seizure in unrelated criminal prosecutions, or only if they agree to contribute $1,000 to the Republican

Party. The customary account strikes down these conditions as irrelevant to the exercise of state power. The obvious fear is that people are too willing to yield rights that are worth little to them in the abstract in order to gain the valuable permission to use the highways. Once everyone yields, the state has leveraged a set of highway rules to undo basic constitutional protections against arbitrary state power or political favoritism. No system of constitutional rights could survive without some version of the unconstitutional conditions doctrine, especially in the modern social democratic state where the government assumes so many functions.

This doctrine plays a vital role in routine land use transactions. More specifically, Scalia saw no proper connection between the state's legitimate interest in creating a "view spot" easement from the PCH over the Nollans' land and the lateral easement in front of their house. He further held that the lateral easement constituted a permanent physical taking that is per se—that is, "in itself, without more"—compensable. He thus refused to allow any public body to manipulate its permit process to get a valuable lateral easement for free. He also balked at sacrificing the rights of the driving public for the benefit of the walking public, when the two "public" groups did not perfectly overlap. Justice Brennan's dissent gloomily predicted that Scalia's decision would induce the Coastal Commission to deny all rebuilding permits, leaving both the public and the landowner worse off than before—which is more or less what happened. In an ironic role reversal, Justice Scalia rejected the principle of freedom of contract that Justice Brennan, uncharacteristically, willingly embraced.

Unfortunately, both Scalia and Brennan labored under a common error, namely, that restrictive covenants on land use don't count as property interests. Reject that assumption, so that physical and regulatory takings receive parallel treatment, and the

Coastal Commission no longer has any incentive to bundle the surrender of lateral easements with the grant of building permits. Without question, the state would have had to compensate the Nollans if it took a lateral easement for public use. What Scalia missed is that the public covenant that allows all persons on the PCH to overlook the Nollans' land operates identically with a private restrictive covenant that gives a neighbor the same right. Accordingly, the state can impose the covenant only if it pays for the lost value, unless it justifies its use under the police power, which it can't in this case. Private law treats the easement and the covenant under the unified law of "servitudes"—the rights that people have over the lands of others. As noted earlier, these come in two forms: covenants typically place restrictions on the use of land above and beyond what the law normally allows. Easements allow the use of someone else's land in ways that would otherwise be a trespass. In all cases that arise in private settings, both easements and covenants have to be acquired by purchase. The parity principle says the state should do the same.

Treating these easements and covenants in the same fashion drains all the mystery out of *Nollan*. To see why, first note that the choice granted by the Coastal Commission did not free it of the charge of state coercion. If the robber tells his victim "Give me your money or I'll take your life," no one treats the money paid over as a gift. Rather, the robber has used coercion by forcing the victim to choose between two entitlements when he should be able to keep both. Civilization would halt if a procession of thugs could demand first your watch, then your wallet, and then the shirt off your back to save your life. Criminal sanctions are needed against threats disguised as choices.

The Coastal Commission played the identical game in *Nollan*, which explains why Scalia was right to use the extortion metaphor. The state offered the Nollans the Hobson's choice between a restrictive covenant and the lateral easement, when the Nollans were entitled to both. Where Scalia went wrong was to assume that something turns on the physical nature of the easement. The same coercive game arises if the state says you may build an extra story but only if you set back your project an extra 10 feet from the road. It does not matter that both restrictions go to use. In both settings, the state rigs the exaction game so that the landowner surrenders the interest that he values less so that the state gets the interest that it values more.

Now note the catch. The bundling distorts the state's process of deciding whether it should condemn any private interests in private land. It does so because it allows the state to escape the discipline that the price system normally imposes on all parties. We know what the easement was worth on the numbers given—it was worth only $75,000 to the state but cost the Nollans $100,000. The state would never purchase that easement in an unbundled transaction. But it will get that easement through bundling, because the only operative comparison asks the Nollans to decide between losing $400,000 for the new house or $100,000 for the easement. The bundling leads to an inefficient land use choice that reduces overall value by $25,000. Bundled offers reveal no social information about the social desirability of having the state take the easement. Unbundled offers force the commission to compare the social with the private value of the easement. The bundled comparison is irrelevant to social welfare. The unbundled comparison is required by it. Yet no harm is done if the easement is worth more in public than in private hands. Thus if the easement is worth $150,000 to the state and costs only $100,000, the state just buys the easement for $100,000.

In sum, the bundling technique is always illegitimate. If the commission had to pay market prices for either or both property interests, it would never give the landowner a free option to compel the commission to purchase either the easement or the covenant at market value. The commission would surely make its own judgment as to which it wanted, given its budgetary constraints. The bundling game looks respectable only because covenants that restrict the ordinary use of land have been wrongly expelled from the catalogue of property interests protected by the takings clause.

ROUGH PROPORTIONALITY

The Supreme Court started down the right path on exactions for the wrong reasons in *Nollan*. Yet that case left open the question of what conditions could be properly imposed. In the 1994 case of *Dolan v. City of Tigard*, the city told the Dolans they could expand their country store and adjacent parking lot only on two conditions. They had to dedicate a portion of their land to improve local drainage, and they had to dedicate about 7,000 square feet of land, or 10 percent of their property, to the city to build a bicycle path to relieve downtown road congestion. Chief Justice Rehnquist insisted on an "essential nexus" between a legitimate state interest and the two exactions, as measured by a "rough proportionality" between risks generated by the proposed development and the exaction directed toward it.

This approach only works by tightly tying the analysis to the antinuisance account of the police power. So understood, the Dolans do *not* receive a clean bill of health, because paving over more of their land reduces absorption and increases the flood risk to downhill properties. The drainage requirement functions like a public injunction to prevent a future downhill harm. The matter, however, is complicated because much runoff comes from upstream lands. The right analysis allows the state, without compensation, to impose conditions to prevent the Dolan runoff, but requires compensation to the extent that the drainage conditions are used to deal with the runoff from upstream owners, or from natural sources. The Dolans pay for their share; other neighbors pay for theirs; and general revenues cover natural flow. In contrast, the dedication for a bicycle path looks like a rerun of the lateral easement in *Nollan*, except in the unlikely event that the expansion of the Dolan's business imposed a disproportionate burden on public streets. But if this occurred, the right response is not a bicycle path into the woods but street widening or off-street parking.

As with other police power questions, the Supreme Court's muddy and inconclusive analysis of exactions has, unfortunately, allowed lower courts to sanction major abuses of the exaction process, thereby forcing newcomers to finance infrastructure improvements that benefit all members of the community. Thus many courts have allowed municipal governments to charge new builders with the cost of financing art museums, refurbishing railroad stations, setting up low-income housing, providing daycare centers, starting job training programs, and anything else that bears some loose "causal nexus" to the new project at hand. This "welcome stranger" ethic sometimes leads to abandoned or delayed projects, with real losses to the individuals who are kept out of the community. In other cases, projects do go forward with a bewildering array of cross-subsidies and factional intrigue that reduces the tax base and the project's overall utility. The correct approach forces developers to respond to nuisances they create or the undue burdens they place on infrastructure, just as they did in *Dolan*, but not otherwise to subsidize public programs for the community at large.

Part IV   Other Applications

CHAPTER ELEVEN

Rate Regulation

BUSINESSES "AFFECTED WITH THE PUBLIC INTEREST"

This examination of takings law has been largely confined to real estate and various forms of personal property. This last part of the book supplements that analysis with a brief overview of two further issues. This chapter discusses various forms of rate regulation that set maximum or minimum prices for the sale of different goods and services. Chapter 12 applies the takings analysis to intellectual property.

Rate regulation occurs in rent control, but the practice has broad application to many businesses, such as electricity, communications, transportation, banking, agriculture, and insurance. The legal issues have often been decided under the due process clauses in the Fifth and Fourteenth Amendments that provide that neither the United States nor the state can take property— the word "private" does not appear—without due process of law. In the late nineteenth century, the Supreme Court held that the words "due process of law" included "without just compensation" in the context of ratemaking proceedings.

That tight connection between the two phrases is perfectly apt, because the rights over private property include the right to dispose of property at whatever price the owner sees fit. That right to dispose is necessarily limited by either maximum or minimum rates. The key question is whether those rate restrictions can be sustained under the police power. Nuisance prevention is not relevant to rate cases, so the inquiry turns necessarily on whether some defect in market structure justifies state regulation. The traditional accounts of rate regulation located that market defect in the firm's monopoly position, whether created either by state franchise or by natural circumstance. The former occurs, for example, when the state grants an exclusive franchise to sell a particular good in a given geographical market. A natural monopoly arises when, for example, a local harbor is large enough to accommodate only a single pier. The traditional body of law, which held sway in the United States until the 1930s, held that rate regulation was proper only for businesses that were "affected by the public interest," which, with only minor exceptions, covered firms that held monopoly power, that is, were the only provider in a given market. All businesses that operated in a competitive environment had a right to charge what the market would bear.

This doctrine originated in the early English common law, dating back at least to the late seventeenth century, if not earlier. One conspicuous illustration is the 1810 case of *Allnut v. Inglis*, which held that the operator of a designated customhouse could not charge whatever it pleased, but only a reasonable and non-discriminatory rate for its services. By statute, goods stored in the customhouse could be shipped to foreign destinations free of all tax on imports destined for domestic use. If the customhouse owner could charge what he pleased, his rates could partially negate the statutory tax relief the government was using to lure shippers to English ports. Forcing reasonable rates meant that the customhouse could charge only what other storage facilities charged for identical goods stored elsewhere for the domestic market—an easy enough inquiry.

This doctrine was explicitly carried over to the United States in the 1876 Supreme Court decision of *Munn v. Illinois*, which sustained the maximum rates that grain elevators used to store goods for shipment by rail could charge to their customers. The Court did not examine the adequacy of the rates, but held that this matter was properly decided by the political branches of government. Enigmatically, the Court only held that the grain elevators held a "virtual monopoly," so it was unclear whether that Court would have extended rate regulation to competitive industries. Within a generation, however, the Supreme Court decided to subject at least some rate regulation to review. To do so, it had to address key questions. First, which firms had the monopoly power under the "affected with the public interest test" and were therefore subject to regulation? Second, what form of regulation was appropriate for them?

On the first question, all competitive industries were exempt from this system of regulation. Owing to the large number of sellers in the marketplace, no seller could charge higher prices to one customer than to others. The disgruntled customers would just shift to another competitor if the seller tried to charge higher rates. Seeing no abuse, the traditional view allowed for no regulation. That result makes sense, given the strong efficiency properties of competitive markets. That position, however, in time eroded under an unrelenting Progressive critique that feared market domination by large firms even in competitive industries.

The difference matters. The traditional view did not allow for rate regulation of the insurance industry, for while the firms were large, they were also numerous, so that competitive conditions prevailed. To the Progressives, the size of individual firms and the total volume of business within the industry justified rate regulation regardless of market structure.

After much irresolution, the traditional doctrine finally collapsed with the Court's 1934 decision in *Nebbia v. New York*, which made it a crime for any grocery store to sell milk at less than 9 cents per quart. Justice Roberts no longer saw rate regulation solely as a counterweight to monopoly power. Rather, he permitted its use to create dairy cartels that both restricted output and raised prices. The new rationale for rate regulation abandoned its original antimonopoly rationale and, ironically, created by statute the same kind of cartel arrangements the antitrust laws are intended to control. The antitrust law attacks private cartels that break down because of cheating. The new statutes invoke state power to fortify these cartels, by preventing the cheating from happening. These statutes hardly take from the firms who are benefited by the restrictions, but they do take from the firms that are excluded from entering the market or from consumers who must pay the higher prices or exit the market.

In other cases, firms are subject to maximum price controls. These controls—such as the price controls on oil and gas in the 1970s—create persistent shortages, as low state prices stimulate demand and reduce supply. Queues and black market activities often result. Both forms of regulation have deleterious consequences. The consequent reduction in overall wealth makes it impossible for the winners to supply just compensation to the losers. The proper rule bans all forms of rate regulation in competitive markets. Restoring the old doctrine would impose a welcome limit on state power.

TECHNIQUES OF REGULATION

Natural Monopolies

The second question deals with identifying the kinds of rate regulation that are appropriate for firms with monopoly power. The standard literature regards rate regulation as appropriate for industries that have economies of scale, that is, those industries for which, over the range of their expected output, additional units of production are always cheaper than the initial units of production. Under these circumstances, a single firm (the "natural monopolist") can always satisfy the entire market at a cost lower than any two or more firms. Accordingly, the first entrant has a huge advantage, because it can always undercut a new entrant, which has to face higher initial per unit prices to get its business off the ground. Yet since the new entrants cannot come in, the natural monopolist can raise its costs above the competitive level without losing its business.

Those price increases result in social waste in at least two ways. First, they exclude from the market any customer who is willing to pay the competitive but not the monopoly price. Second, they encourage the dominant firm to practice price discrimination in ways that are unrelated to the costs of providing service, by charging high demanders more for identical goods than low demanders. The system of rate regulation is intended, by incurring both error and administrative costs, to limit the natural monopolist to competitive prices.

These benefits from rate regulation are paired with serious weaknesses. First, it is hard to work the system correctly, even with the best of intentions. Uniform prices for all customers, for example, could lead to unwanted cross-subsidies (whereby one customer pays for goods consumed by another) if the cost of supplying each is different. Regulation therefore has to allow for what are termed "cost justified" differences. These regulations are costly to implement and often lead to unintended rigidities. A very respectable body of opinion thinks that allowing new technologies to erode natural monopolies outperforms even intelligent regulation.

That position has little constitutional traction, so rate regulation is routinely allowed if a legislature so chooses. But its decisions cannot be free of constitutional restraint. Once the natural monopolist invests heavily in infrastructure by laying track, pipe, or wire, it is vulnerable to state regulation that specifies rates high enough to recover its ("variable") costs of doing future business, but not high enough to recoup the original capital costs needed to set up the railroad, gas, or communication grid. No firm will make that investment if left unprotected against confiscation by regulation. The takings law allows the state regulation to eliminate monopoly profits, but not to prevent the firm from recovering the costs of its front-end investment, with reasonable return adjusted to the level of risk.

Two Forms of Rate Regulation

Historically, the problem came to a head in the 1898 case of *Smyth v. Ames*, in which the Supreme Court struck down a Nebraska statute that uniformly cut the rates on railroad transportation by nearly 30 percent, without determining that those rates let the railroads recover its cost of capital. In setting the legal standard, any inquiry has to focus on two principal variables. The first asks what outlays are properly included in the rate base. The second asks about the allowable rate of return on that base. On the first question, *Smyth* held that the regulated industry could only recover for those expenditures that produced assets that were "used and usable" for the firm. Under this formula, the railroads could not include within their rate base any expenditures that were adjudged to be wasted or mistaken. Because the railroads took the risk of the smaller rate base, they received as compensation a higher rate of return on the assets included in that smaller base.

Justice Douglas adopted the opposite position in *Federal Power Commission v. Hope Natural Gas*, decided in 1944. Douglas despaired of making any accurate reckoning to decide which of the myriad expenditures were proper and which were not. So he included all actual capital expenditures in the rate base, but lowered the effective rate of return because the public utility assumed fewer risks. His sole inquiry looked to the "bottom line." If the regulated industry made its needed rate of return, the courts would not examine any errors in classifying individual items of revenue or expense.

The choice between *Smyth* and *Hope* is not easy. Even if *Hope* eliminates the thorny problem of measuring the rate base, it creates an incentive for the regulated firm to inefficiently pad its rate base. In the absence of any clear verdict as to which weakness dominates, the Supreme Court in the 1989 decision in *Duquesne Light v. Barasch* essentially gave the government the option to select either system. That decision denied Duquesne its investments in an initially authorized nuclear power plant whose completion had been first delayed and then canceled for various reasons, including the Arab Oil embargo and the nuclear accident at Three Mile Island (also in Pennsylvania). The reasons, however, did not include any new-found defect in the original plans or other mistake in performance by Duquesne. Chief Justice Rehnquist held that the *retroactive* rate denial was permissible so long as the utility's overall rate of return remained at an acceptable level under *Hope*.

On balance his decision seems wrong. Stability of expectations is the hallmark of property rights. Even if the financial rate of return to Duquesne remained high enough under the *Hope* test, after the retroactive reduction, it was still unwise to allow it. Any prospect of some unknown downward revision in future rates introduces an unnecessary uncertainty into the business calculations. That struggle does not lead to better performance, but only shrinks the total gains available to all through struggle between the shareholders and ratepayers over the distribution of the spoils. The *Duquesne* rule also encourages government agencies to disallow particular expenses when the earlier rates turn out to be more profitable than expected. At the same time, it permits these agencies to do nothing when the designated rates turn out to be low. Denying regulators the right to retroactive adjustments without cause averts these risks, and induces more thoughtful ratemaking in the first place, without raising the endless disputes over line items that led to the adoption of the *Hope* rule.

Telecommunications

The greatest danger of allowing retroactive adjustments is that it eases the path to making compromises in the basic ratemaking methodology. Just this happened in Federal Communications Commission (FCC) ratemaking under the Telecommunications Act of 1996. This Act required the incumbent Regional Bell Operating Companies (RBOCs), who enjoyed statutory monopolies over local telephone service in their communities, to give free options to any potential competitors to purchase components of their networks at prices set by the FCC. The RBOCs had made huge investments in their networks, which rapidly depreciated over time. The governing statute required the FCC to set its prices relative to cost, without specifying that these costs were the actual historical costs incurred in setting up the network. The FCC set these rates based on (lower) cost to assemble an ideal network at some later time when a compulsory sale of these components to a new entrant took place. This pricing system required the RBOCs to absorb all the interim network depreciation. The bottom line was this: if the incumbents sold off all networks piece by piece to new entrants, they could not recover their historical costs.

The Supreme Court held that, as a matter of administrative law, large deference had to be given to the FCC in setting rates. It upheld the rate structure even though it did not provide full compensation for the components sold. That ruling was not challenged on constitutional grounds, because it was evident that the Court would adopt the same deferential position. Even so, the decision flouts sound constitutional principles. In essence, the FCC pricing rules gave a low rate of return on a narrow rate base. Its approach thus combines the most restrictive features of *Smyth* and *Hope Natural Gas*. That combination justified invalidating the entire program as an uncompensated taking. As ever, improper pricing formulas led to untoward social effects. Even with their free option to purchase components at below cost, no new entrant could achieve a strong competitive position, given that other new entrants could buy components at the same low rates. Both the incumbents and the new entrants alike lost several hundred billion dollars in the process. The entire episode could have been avoided at far lower cost by removing from the 1996 Act the option to buy components at administratively set rates. Instead, the new entrants could have been required (at less cost) to build out their own networks under FCC rules that facilitated interconnection with the established firms, so that any telephone subscriber from any company could contact any other subscriber from any other company. The sober lesson from land use regulation carries over to rate regulation. The ability of the government to force exchanges leads to major abuses when it chooses the wrong prices. Yet proper pricing won't happen so long as courts ignore the just compensation requirement. The strong political pressures to give low short-term rates to consumers will cloud the process, and deter long-term innovation.

CHAPTER TWELVE

Intellectual Property

CREATING RIGHTS

The four main areas of intellectual property are patents, copyright, trade secrets, and trade names, each subject to distinct legal regimes at the federal and state level. All four areas, however, have two common threads. First, ordinary language, natural laws, and simple ideas receive no intellectual property protection but fall into the public domain. No one can patent the Pythagorean theorem or obtain trademark protection for the word "podcast." Second, all forms of protected intellectual property give the owner some degree of exclusive control over something—an invention, a composition, a symbol, a formula—that has value separate from its physical instantiation. Neither particular books nor computer chips get intellectual property protection, which is reserved for the exclusive right to make the invention or print the book.

The key question is whether, and if so, how, intellectual property rights receive protection under the takings clause. The answer comes in two parts. First, the federal government, which has exclusive jurisdiction to create patents and copyrights for limited times, is under no obligation to create either. Congress could choose to have all inventions and writings fall into the public domain. The rules are known, and authors and inventors have to play by them. In contrast, ordinary people can unilaterally generate trade secrets simply by keeping some valuable item like an industrial process or a customer list secret. Typically state law defines the legal protection given to these secrets when used or licensed under confidentiality agreements. That protection, however, never prevents someone else from making the independent discovery of the same secret, and in any event, trade secret protection typically ends when the secret is disclosed. Trademarks, which are governed by both state and federal law, typically last forever and are protected by both damages and injunctions. Once again, Congress and the states need not create this form of property, but they invariably do so because of the enormous boon to commerce.

PROTECTING AND CONDITIONING RIGHTS

The result is different after particular intellectual property rights have been created under federal or state law. The takings issues for intellectual property have precise physical analogs. First, in principle, any distinction between a physical and a regulatory taking could be rejected with intellectual property, so that any loss of the right to exclude, use, or dispose could be prima facie compensable to the extent of the owner's diminution in value. But if that distinction is accepted with real property, it easily carries over to the intellectual property universe. If the government only *restricts* how the intellectual property holder uses his right, then there is a regulatory taking, which should be evaluated under the tripartite test of *Penn Central*. But where the law actually allows someone else to *use* the intellectual property, the per se takings rules should apply, whether or not the original owner may continue to exploit his writing, invention, secret, or mark. One obvious application of the rule is to trigger compensation if the government authorizes a generic manufacturer to make a licensed pharmaceutical whose patent period has not yet run. To date, the case law on this point is unclear, but it is possible that this per se rule will eventually be adopted, notwithstanding the tempting rhetorical argument that there can be no physical takings of intellectual property rights. What matters is that the use of the intellectual property by the state or others acting under its authorization is just like the use of any physical asset, and therefore should trigger, even under current law, the per se obligation to compensate.

Second, under *Penn Central*, the holder of an intellectual property right faces an uphill battle to gain compensation unless he is deprived of all rights of use. But the question of restrictions on the right to sell, as with pharmaceutical price controls, is more complicated under the usual rules on ratemaking. The first query is whether the rate base for drugs includes the dry holes from pharmaceutical research, as it surely should. Second, in light of the explicit patent bargain that gives unfettered price control for a limited time, any rate regulation necessarily leaves the patent holder worse off than before. Similar problems arise if federal regulation forces patentees to license their products to competitors in exchange for a mandated royalty fee. Again under the parity principle, if the compulsory licenses do not generate firm revenues equal to those that could be derived from selling the patented good in an unregulated market, the takings claim looks attractive in theory, for otherwise there is no obvious limit on the power of the Congress to renege on its outstanding patent grants. But the issue is still unsettled.

Third, government exactions may be deployed with patents, copyrights, and trade secrets. For example, Congress could decree that the intellectual property holder will receive a license to market a drug or insecticide only if it agrees to share its property with its competitors. Initially, it is unquestionable that the receipt of a patent only gives the exclusive right to sell, but does not insulate the patentee from the need to require Food and Drug Administration (FDA) approval. Indeed, under the 1984 Hatch Waxman Act, Congress granted patent holders limited extensions of their patent period as a partial offset to the time lost before the FDA. But the term extension does not add one additional day for each day lost before the FDA. Instead it adds one day back for two days lost before the FDA, but caps the additional length of term at thirty months. With ever longer periods in clinical trials, this period does not come close to allowing effective patent use for the full patent term. The exact period for effective drug commercialization today will vary from drug to drug, depending on the length of the FDA proceedings. But the average useful commercial life today is under ten years, or less than half the basic patent life of twenty years.

In many cases, moreover, regulators create still greater problems because their exactions have little or nothing to do with either health or safety. For example, in the 1984 case of *Ruckelshaus v. Monsanto Inc.*, the Supreme Court first held that trade secrets were protected under the takings law because they were a species of property that was recognized under state law. But the protection that the decision extended was sharply curtailed by this caveat: Congress could force a trade secret holder to reveal its secrets to a competitor in order to obtain the license to sell its product in the United States. If the trade secret holder did not like the condition, then it could sell overseas. The net effect of this rule was that the state's legitimate concern with health and safety could be leveraged in order to make the information in a trade secret a public good, which of course reduces the incentive of people to invest in trade secrets in the first place. That cavalier treatment of property rights stands in manifest tension with the *Nollan* decision on lateral easements that the Supreme Court decided in the next year, and to this day it is uncertain whether this truncation of trade secrets represents current law.

In principle, however, there is no real difficulty with this matter, even under current law. The key point in the analysis is this: the distinction between physical and regulatory takings gives the government the benefit of a low standard of review from the *Penn Central* case whenever it only *restricts* a private owner's use of property without making any use of that property itself. But the moment the government *uses* the property or authorizes its use by others, then compensation is judged under a virtual per se, or automatic rule applicable to physical takings. Even though no public or private party can "occupy" a trade secret in the same way it can occupy land, this distinction still carries over from the land cases. Where the government only restricts a private party's use of its trade secret, it gets the benefit of the low *Penn Central* standard of review, which gives every break to the government. But if, as in *Monsanto,* it uses the trade secret itself, or authorizes its use by a competitor, then the per se standard should apply. Any rules that are applicable for land or other tangible assets should carry over to trade secrets or other forms of intellectual property like trademarks, patents, and copyrights.

Finally, takings arguments are made to resist efforts to *expand* the scope of intellectual property rights. In particular, the 1998 Copyright Term Extension Act just added twenty years to existing copyrights, an enormous windfall for patents with a year or so to run. That decision conflicts with the customary argument that treats the patent term solely as a reward for the innovation that generated the copyright. A respectable argument could be made that by lengthening the term, Congress takes the right of all individuals to make use of what should have become a public domain resource. Nonetheless, in 2003, the Supreme Court in *Eldred v. Ashcroft* applied its usual deferential standard to hold that Congress had virtually unlimited power to extend the terms of copyrights and, by implication, patents.

This brief overview reveals that the same deferential trend that defines the takings law for tangible property applies to intellectual property as well, which makes these rights less secure than they ought to be. Yet given the large congressional role in defining patents and copyrights, the constitutional arguments count for less going forward. What truly matters is a Congress and Supreme Court that are alert to the long-term social losses that follow from the destabilization of the system of intellectual property rights.

CHAPTER THIRTEEN

Final Reflections

ECONOMIC LIBERTIES

The major purpose of this book is to explain why the faithful constitutional protection of private property is not some parochial exercise, but is an indispensable part of any comprehensive constitutional order that advances long-term social welfare. The generative power of its analysis derives from a single conceptual framework that covers the interactions between the individual and the state with respect to all forms of property rights. As noted in the beginning of chapter 6, the key questions are:

(1) Was private property taken, either by occupation or by restrictions on use or disposition? If so,

(2) was that taking justified under the police power to protect against wrongs that the property owner committed against others? If not,

(3) was that taking for a public use? If not, then the consent of the owner is needed. If so,

(4) was just compensation paid by the state to the owner for the full losses incurred by the taking?

These principles have complete universality. They apply to interests in land, extend to common pool assets like fish and game or oil and gas, and from there to complex matters pertaining to rate regulation and intellectual property. Nor is this basic framework limited to matters of property, with its strong economic overtones. The same analysis carries over to various forms of economic liberties, including the right to work any lawful occupation. Here the relevant issues have a familiar ring. First, can the state take away that right to enter into personal agreements for the sale or use of labor? Yes, in principle, but only if it respects the same limitations applicable in private property cases. Thus the state can stop agreements that harm third persons through violence or monopoly. It may take steps to protect contracting parties against fraud and incompetence. But it should not be allowed to impose restrictions on wages or terms of service unrelated to these interests.

This overall conclusion is no modest prescription, in light of the extensive regulation of labor markets that is the hallmark of the modern post–New Deal state. But it nonetheless is sound in principle. Regardless of their lofty pretensions, minimum wage, collective bargaining, and antidiscrimination laws are subject to the same challenges that can be lodged against various restrictions on the use of land or other forms of private property. The acid test is whether the import of the regulation is to protect rivals from competition by the regulated entities or to protect individuals from exploitation, as is commonly supposed.

There is, historically, a close intellectual affinity between stronger protection of economic liberties that was the constitutional norm before 1937 and the analysis of the takings clause I have offered here. The key case is the now infamous five-to-four decision of the Supreme Court in *Lochner v. New York* (1905) that struck down a New York criminal statute that forbade certain types of bakery employees from working more than ten hours per day or sixty hours per week. The decision is widely reviled because it is said to strip the state of power to protect helpless individual workers from the ravages of industrialization, just as zoning laws are said to protect communities from overdevelopment. But just whom were these statutes protecting? The conventional account holds that it was Lochner's employees. But the case itself was a criminal prosecution in which none of the workers complained of their working conditions. How, therefore, were they protected by a rule that limited their occupational choices on the supposed ground that the state knew their interests better than they did? Do the same workers really return to the same jobs day after day without realizing the errors of their ways? And it is in general not credible to think that labor markets systematically fail when the unbroken historical trend during the Progressive Era in the absence of employment regulation was an across-the-board reduction in working hours and accident rates, coupled with an increase in real wages.

In practice, maximum hours regulation had nothing to do with health and safety and everything to do with the limitation of competition, in this instance with union bakers. How do we know that this was the case? Because of the disparate impact of a facially neutral regulation—the same test of such importance in land use cases. The subsection in the New York statute before the maximum hour limitation required employers to supply adequate ventilation in sleeping quarters. That odd provision was inserted because small bakers such as Lochner used a single shift of workers to bake the bread in the evening and later to prepare it for shipment in the morning. In between, they slept on the job; hence the long hours. The neutral ten-hour regulation did nothing to interfere with the operation of the unionized shops, because those workers did not exceed that limit. But this neutral regulation worked a tremendous disruption on Lochner's operation, since his bakers did work shifts longer than ten hours, even if they slept part-time on the job. The New York statute thus exceeds any rational conception of the police power, for its major purpose was not safety, but to alter the competitive balance between competitive firms. The cardinal virtue, therefore, of the much-reviled *Lochner* decision was that it preserved the operation of competitive labor markets from the corrosive effects of differential state regulation. The police power was idle, because there was no market imperfection to cure.

RELIGION AND SPEECH

The basic four-part approach defended in this book also resonates in all constitutional cases of individual rights. There is first an inquiry as to how far the basic right goes. Consider, for example, the specific protections for noneconomic interests such as religion and speech. Does speech cover all forms of communication, including not only art and theater but also nude dancing or sleeping in a public park in silent protest? Does any set of cosmic beliefs, however eccentric, count as religion? Once these boundary conditions are settled, the intellectual framework developed in the takings cases carries over without missing a beat. What is the scope of the police power, both with respect to the choice of ends and means? It may well be proper to limit speech that poses an imminent threat to social peace and political order, but not speech that advocates peaceful change to a system of democratic socialism through electoral politics. Similarly, the state can enjoin the operation of a public nuisance, but it cannot simply designate so-called adult theaters as nuisances that can be shut down by the state. Nor can the state treat other activities like flag-burning or private sexual conduct as nuisances, even when others *rightly* find them offensive or unpatriotic. Religions may espouse repellent beliefs or engage in offensive rituals, but they cannot sacrifice anyone's children, emit pollution, or torture animals.

The renewed reliance on the classical liberal scheme arises because the Supreme Court justices *care* about the rights protected. The critical variable is the level of scrutiny brought. Whenever strict or intermediate scrutiny is applied to speech or religion cases, as is commonly the case, the judges use the *exact* framework they reject in takings cases to determine whether the state can justify the abridgment of the constitutional right. They refuse to budge beyond the classical liberal definition of the police power to give additional running room to state power.

Nonetheless, the judges are not pure libertarians when it comes to thinking about speech and religion. Their regulation of natural monopolies means that the police power is not limited to the control of force and fraud. The state that can stop firms from polluting can also prevent them from colluding on prices. If the Supreme Court had upheld the strong protection of economic liberties, it would have struck down all mandatory regimes of collective bargaining, so that newspapers would not have to seek, but fail to gain, a freedom from unions whose work rules "incidentally," as modern courts like to say, can block journalistic innovation by raising costs and reducing job flexibility.

TAXATION

A similar analysis applies to taxation. Although there was no space to develop the point in the main text, the rigorous view of the takings clause does not preclude all taxation, as in some libertarian fantasy world, but it does militate strongly to a flat tax favored by Adam Smith as the best means to limit government's discretion, and hence abuse, without limiting its ability to meet the revenue target of its choice. Lo and behold, this issue plays out precisely that way under the First Amendment, which for just these reasons prevents the state from using progressive taxes on income, or other forms of special taxation to favor small over large newspapers.

Surprisingly, this framework even applies to key structural issues within our federal system. Our national commitment to free trade across state lines prohibits independent state action adopted for protectionist reasons. The competitive markets that are spurned in property and economic liberty cases are treated as the constitutional gold standard. In good police power fashion, state restrictions on cross-border transactions must be directed to serious physical harms that cannot be controlled by lesser means. Otherwise, the current law looks askance at state laws with a disproportionate impact on out-of-state interests. The fear of externalities and faction that is so blithely ignored in the area of takings law fortunately dominates this area today with only modest slippage.

This quick overview of adjacent areas should dispel the illusion that a reinvigorated takings law is hopelessly ahistorical, idiosyncratic, idealistic, or unworkable. To the contrary, that framework, which is used today with success in other areas, offers the only clear path out of our current constitutional morass. I believe this approach is consistent with the letter and spirit of the constitutional text, and its faithful application offers the best chance at controlling the factional abuses inherent in any system of democratic politics. Politically, a major constitutional transformation is not in the cards today, which is a shame. But in the short run, a keen awareness of the dangers of the current system may well influence incrementally the character of political decisions at all levels of government for the better. But in the long run, we should not settle for the current backhanded treatment that property rights receive at the hands of our courts and legislatures. Rather, we should redouble our efforts to bring the needed coherence and clarity to the articulation of a set of sound constitutional provisions governing private property. These principles are no antiquarian wonder whose time has come and gone. They are needed now, and needed more than ever. We have paid a heavy social price for the manifest neglect that the Supreme Court has shown to the first principles that should govern the use of the government's power to take and to regulate.

Index

. . .

ownership (*continued*)
  government reducing, 53–54
  legal system and, 19
  regulations challenged with, 109
  single individual sufficient for,
    17–18
  split, 109
  takings clause protection
    of, 90–91

Pacific Coast Highway (PCH),
  137
parity principle, 55–58
  compensable taking under, 118
  courts violating, 125
  physical takings and, 55–56
  property possession regained
    by, 70
partial condemnation, 93–94
patent holder extensions, 38
PCH. *See* Pacific Coast Highway
Penn Central Company, 119–20
Penn Central v. City of New York,
  120, 123–26
Pennsylvania Coal Co. v. Mahon,
  105
Pennsylvania, mineral leases in,
  105–7
permanent/temporary takings,
  129–30
personal rights, 17
physical invasions, 55–73
physical occupation, 124–25
physical takings
  by government, 56–57
  intellectual property rejected
    by, 158–59

issues of, 55
landowner property lost due to,
  53–54
mechanics of, 54
multiple interests influencing,
  65
parity principle and, 55–56
regulatory takings clause v.,
  97–99
rent control statues and, 69–70
Supreme court decisions on, 50
*Poletown Neighborhood Council v.
  City of Detroit,* 81–82
police power, 6–7, 98
  assessment of, 118
  government takings and,
    130–31
  public use v., 128
  risk assumption and, 108–10
political coalition, landowner's,
  103–4
political safeguards, 100
pollution, 130–31
power
  concentration of, 29
  divided, 36–37
preservation
  environmental, 130–31
  of landmarks, 119–23
  ordinance, 122
  statues, 119–23
pricing formulas, improper, 155
"prima facie," 41
primitive societies, 15–16
principle of reciprocity, 23–24
prisoner's dilemma, 59
private enforcement, 27

Index of Cases

· · ·